Do Our Children Have a Chance?

Do Our Children Have a Chance?

A Human Opportunity Report for Latin America and the Caribbean

José R. Molinas Vega
Ricardo Paes de Barros
Jaime Saavedra Chanduvi
Marcelo Giugale
with Louise J. Cord, Carola Pessino, and Amer Hasan

THE WORLD BANK
Washington, D.C.

ISBN (paper): 978-0-8213-8699-6
ISBN (electronic): 978-0-8213-8902-7
DOI: 10.1596/978-0-8213-8699-6

Library of Congress Cataloging-in-Publication Data
Do our children have a chance? : the human opportunity report for Latin America and the Caribbean / José R. Molinas Vega ... [et al.].
    p. cm.
  Includes bibliographical references and index.
  ISBN 978-0-8213-8699-6 — ISBN 978-0-8213-8902-7 (electronic)
  1. Children—Latin America—Social conditions. 2. Children—Latin America—Economic conditions. 3. Children—Caribbean Area—Social conditions. 4. Children—Caribbean Area—Economic conditions. I. Molinas, Jose R., 1966-
  HQ792.L3D62 2011
  305.23098—dc23

                                                                    2011038591

Cover image: Road photo by Daniel Zamora/SXC; child photo and photo illustration by Ari Ribas and Ane Castro
Cover design: Naylor Design and Quantum Think

Contents

Boxes

Figures

Tables

Acknowledgments

Do Our Children Have a Chance? A Human Opportunity Report for Latin America and the Caribbean is the result of a collaborative effort that brought together a team of professionals from within and outside the World Bank. The report was prepared under the guidance of Louise J. Cord (World Bank) and Marcelo Giugale (World Bank) by a team led by José R. Molinas Vega (World Bank). Team members included Ricardo Paes de Barros (IPEA-Brazil), Jaime Saavedra Chanduvi (World Bank), Carola Pessino (UDTD-Argentina), and Amer Hasan (World Bank). The team received valuable support from Joao Pedro Azevedo (World Bank), Eliana Rubiano (World Bank), Carlos Sandoval (World Bank), Gabriel Facchini (World Bank), Ngoc-Bich Tran (World Bank), Samuel Franco (IPEA-Brazil), Andrezza Rosalem (IPEA-Brazil), and Ramiro Soria (UTDT-Argentina). The report was improved by three principal reviewers: Francisco H. G. Ferreira (World Bank), Peter Lanjouw (World Bank), and Emiliana Vegas (World Bank). Juliana Pungiluppi (World Bank) worked on the Spanish translation, and Chris Humphrey served as the editor. Ane Orsi (World Bank) and Ari Ribas (APIS Propoganda e Marketing) produced the cover design. Ane Orsi (World Bank), Lucy Bravo (World Bank), and Anne Pillay (World Bank) were instrumental in the production of the final report.

Although the writing of this report has been a collective effort, the principal authors of the chapters are as follows:

- Overview: Marcelo Giugale
- Chapter 1: Ricardo Paes de Barros, Jaime Saavedra Chanduvi, and José R. Molinas Vega
- Chapter 2: José R. Molinas Vega
- Chapter 3: José R. Molinas Vega and Amer Hasan
- Chapter 4: Carola Pessino

Contributors

José R. Molinas Vega holds a PhD in economics from the University of Massachusetts, Amherst. He is a Senior Economist with the Poverty Reduction and Gender Group in the Latin America and the Caribbean Region at the World Bank.

Ricardo Paes de Barros holds a PhD in economics from the University of Chicago and a post-PhD from the International Growth Center at Yale University. He is currently a researcher and the coordinator for the evaluation of public policies at the Instituto de Pesquisa Econômica Aplicada (IPEA).

Jaime Saavedra Chanduvi holds a PhD in economics from Columbia University in New York City. He is the Sector Manager of the Poverty Reduction and Equity Department of the World Bank.

Marcelo Giugale holds a PhD in economics from the London School of Economics. He is Sector Director of the Poverty Reduction and Economic Management Department in the Africa Region at the World Bank.

Louise J. Cord holds a PhD in development and economic policy from the Fletcher School of Law and Diplomacy, at Tufts University. She is Sector Manager of the Poverty Reduction and Gender Group in the Latin America and the Caribbean Region at the World Bank.

Carola Pessino holds a PhD in economics from the University of Chicago. She is a consultant with the World Bank.

Amer Hasan holds a PhD in public policy from the University of Chicago, Harris School of Public Policy Studies. He is a consultant with the Poverty Reduction and Gender Group in the Latin America and the Caribbean Region at the World Bank.

Abbreviations

GDP	gross domestic product
HOI	Human Opportunity Index
IPUMS	Integrated Public Use Microdata Series
LAC	Latin America and the Caribbean
OECD	Organisation for Economic Co-operation and Development
PISA	Programme for International Student Assessment
SN	subnational
SPP	Specific Purpose Payment

Do Our Children Have a Chance? A Human Opportunity Report for Latin America and the Caribbean

Imagine a country where your future does not depend on where you come from, how much your family earns, what color your skin is, or whether you are male or female. Imagine if personal circumstances, those over which you have no control or responsibility, were irrelevant to your opportunities, and to your children's opportunities. And imagine now a statistical tool that can help governments monitor progress toward such a reality. Welcome to the Human Opportunity Index (HOI).

The HOI calculates how personal circumstances (such as birthplace, wealth, race, or gender) impact a child's probability of accessing the services that are necessary to succeed in life, such as timely education, running water, or connection to electricity. It was first published in 2008, applied to Latin America and the Caribbean (LAC). The findings were eye-opening: Behind the enormous inequality that characterizes the region's distribution of development outcomes (income, land ownership, and educational attainment, among others), there is an even more worrying inequality of development opportunities. Not only are rewards unequal, but opportunities are as well. The problem is not just about equality; it is about equity, too. The playing field is uneven from the start.

1

This book reports on the status and evolution of human opportunity in LAC. It builds on the 2008 publication in several directions. First, it uses newly available data to expand the set of opportunities and personal circumstances under analysis. The data are representative of about 200 million children living in 19 countries over the last 15 years. Second, it compares human opportunity in LAC with that of developed countries, among them the United States and France, two very different models of social policy. This allows for illuminating exercises in benchmarking and extrapolation. Third, it looks at human opportunity within countries—across regions, states, and cities. This gives us a preliminary glimpse at the geographic dimension of equity, and at the role that different federal structures play.

The overall message that emerges is one of cautious hope. LAC is making progress in opening the doors of development to all, but it still has a long way to go. At the current pace, it would take, on average, a generation for the region to achieve universal access to just the basic services that make for human opportunity. Seen from the viewpoint of equity, even our most successful nations lag far behind the developed world—and intra-county regional disparities are large and barely converging. Fortunately, there is much policy makers can do about it.

How Does the HOI Work?

In its simplest interpretation, the HOI measures the availability of services that are necessary to progress in life (say, running water), discounted or "penalized" by how unfairly the services are distributed among the population. For example, two countries that have identical coverage may have a different HOI if the citizens that lack the service are all female, or black, or poor, or have many siblings, or, more generally, share a personal circumstance beyond their control (such as family income). In other words, the HOI is coverage corrected for equity. In theory, one can increase it by changing people's circumstances (the "composition effect"), providing more service to all ("scale effect"), or distributing service more fairly ("equalization effect").

The HOI runs from zero to 100; a society that has achieved universal coverage of all services would score at 100. To make comparisons possible across countries and across time, the HOI for LAC presented in this report uses only services and circumstances that are available in all household surveys. Specifically, it looks at access to water, electricity, and sanitation, as well as school enrollment and timely completion of the sixth grade. A rich empirical literature demonstrates that, without those basic services, the chances of a productive life are close to nil. The HOI focuses on seven personal circumstances: parents' education, family income, number of siblings, presence of both parents in the house, gender, gender of household head, and location of residence. In all cases, the unit of focus is the child, defined as an individual between birth and age 16. This isolates the problem of effort and choice—in this age range, children can hardly be responsible for their fate.

Of course, in country-specific applications of the HOI, data availability may allow for more, or more sophisticated, services and circumstances, such as preventive dental check-ups, Internet access, ethnic identification, or father's occupation. Some of that will be shown here, when comparing LAC countries with their developed-world peers.

Is Human Opportunity Expanding in LAC?

Human opportunity is expanding in the region, but slowly and with marked differences across countries. Since 1995, the region's average HOI has grown at a rate of one percentage point per year. This is clearly insufficient. For example, at its current rate, Central America would take 36 years to achieve universality in basic education and housing.

The good news is that all countries have raised their HOI in the last 15 years, some quite rapidly (the fastest improvement occurred in Mexico). Variations remain wide, though, from top-performer Chile (HOI of 95) to Honduras (52). Interestingly, the five countries with the highest HOI—Chile, Uruguay, Mexico, República Bolivariana de Venezuela, and Costa Rica—have very different development models (figure O.1).

Some countries excel at certain services and not at others. For example, Jamaica has the highest educational HOI but is only midtable in housing. Even within type of service, issues of quality arise: LAC children have more chances to be enrolled in school than to complete the sixth grade on time. Enrollment, it seems, is no synonym for learning.

Sadly, personal circumstances still matter greatly for Latin American children. Your parents' level of education will very likely determine yours, and your birthplace is still the most powerful predictor of whether you will have access to basic infrastructure.

LAC governments have, in general, made some progress toward improving equity. The bulk of the new opportunities opened to the region's children came from improved coverage rates for all children (54 percent). Twenty-seven percent of the average improvement in HOI is attributable

Figure O.1   The 2010 HOI for LAC

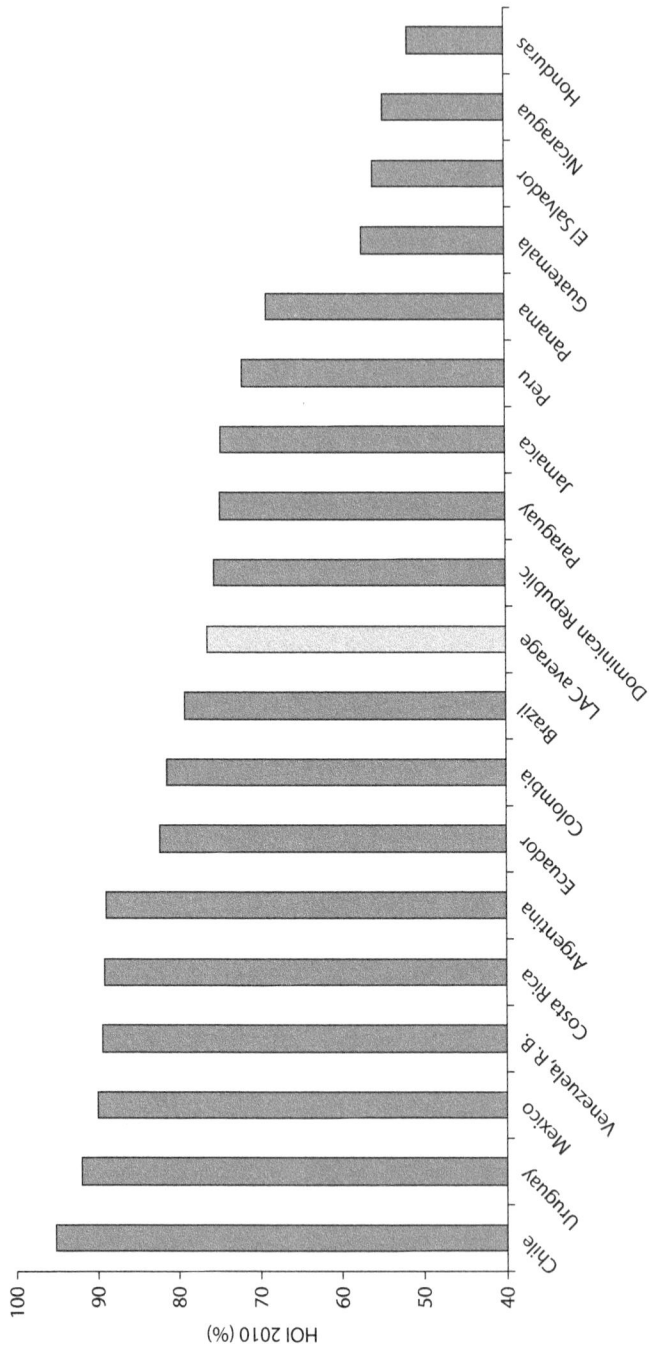

Source: Authors.
Note: LAC = Latin America and the Caribbean.

to a reduction in inequality of opportunity. By contrast, improvements due to changes in the circumstances accounted for only 20 percent of the improvements in the LAC HOI.

Latin America versus Rich Countries

Using standardized test results from the Organisation for Economic Co-operation and Development's Programme for International Student Assessment, and the related demographic data, it is possible to construct an HOI that measures the educational opportunities faced by 15-year-old children around the world. In other words, it is possible to measure how important those children's personal circumstances are in determining their proficiency in reading, mathematics, or science. This sheds an uncomfortable light on LAC. Even the countries with the highest scores in the region, Chile and Uruguay, rank well below the worst-performing countries in Europe and North America. Much of the gap is not due to the fact that rich countries just provide more education services, but to the relatively unfair way in which those services are distributed in LAC. If you are a Latin American student, the wealthier your family is, the better your test results.

A similar exercise can be performed for housing conditions using census data. Again, LAC has work to do: The opportunity of living in a house with sanitation facilities or free from overcrowding is highly dependent on personal circumstances. In both conditions, only a handful of countries in the region score above the European average. Again, this is due less to larger coverage in Europe than to unfair provision in LAC.

Finally, international comparison allows us to peek at how human opportunity could evolve in LAC over the long term. Using a half century's worth of relevant data for the United States and France, an HOI for housing conditions can be built. It shows a clear pattern: rapid initial growth, followed by a marked slow-down, and virtually stalling right before the point of universal coverage. The lesson is clear: The better you do, the harder it is to make progress.

Country, State, City

How is human opportunity distributed at the subnational level? Enough information is at hand to replicate the HOI for about 165 states and cities in LAC, over the last 15 years. The results are telling. First, dispersion is wide among subnationals, with Tierra del Fuego at one end (HOI of

96) and the Atlantic region of Nicaragua at the other (29). Second, all capital cities rank higher than the rest of their countries, and that gap is wider the lower the level of the national HOI.

Third, convergence appears slow, but lagging geographic areas do improve faster and catch up in providing more opportunities to their local population—a mirror image of the observed evolution of human opportunity among countries. Fourth, the bigger or the less decentralized a country is, the more dispersed its regions' HOI appear. Fifth, decentralization seems to have been more effective in diminishing regional inequity, but more so in education than in housing.

What Can Be Done?

LAC remains the most unequal region in the world. The result has been acrimonious political disagreement over the proper role of the state: Should it redistribute wealth or protect private property? Where there is no disagreement, however, is over the need to give all Latin Americans the same opportunities, as a matter of social justice or as a call to personal effort. Although equality is controversial, equity enjoys support across the political spectrum.

Although not discussed in the report, the HOI makes it possible to redirect social policy toward equity (where there is consensus) and away from equality (where there is not). How? Many existing social policies and programs are already equity enhancing, but focusing on equity reveals new points of emphasis along the individual's life cycle. Early interventions, from pregnancy monitoring and institutional births to toddlers' nutrition and neurological development, get a new sense of priority. So do preschool access (such as pre-kindergarten social interaction) and primary school achievement (such as reading standards and critical thinking). The physical security, reproductive education, mentoring, and talent screening of adolescents, all areas that are often overlooked, gain new relevance. A battery of legal and institutional preconditions become sine qua non, from birth certificates, voter registration, and property titles to the enforcement of antidiscrimination, antitrust, and access-to-information laws. Blanket subsidies that, at the margin, are consumed by those who do not need them (free public college education for the rich, to name one) turn into opportunity-wasting aberrations. If anything else, the quest for equity will lead to a final push in the decade-long process of targeting subsidies and will spell the end game for a way of giving out public assistance that was blind to the needs of the recipient—a process that was intrinsically unfair.

At the same time, when applied within countries, the HOI is a powerful tool to identify and address regional inequities. Should not a child-citizen have the same chances in life no matter where in the national territory he or she is born? Several LAC governments in recent years have implemented mechanisms to equalize service provision across subnational jurisdictions. Most of those mechanisms are based on regional factors such as poverty levels, efforts at self-taxation, and ownership of natural resources. The question now is whether equal opportunity among children should not be taken into account too.

CHAPTER 1

How Far Are We from Ensuring Opportunities for All? The Human Opportunity Index

Universal access to key goods and services such as clean water, basic education, health services, minimum nutrition, and citizenship rights is a crucial step toward justice and fairness. Expanding access to these goods and services has long been a central issue in the analysis of economic development and in public policy discussions, including the Millennium Development Goals initiative. The chance people have to pursue the life of their choosing involves the opportunity to access key goods and services, which constitute human capital investments that expand each individual's abilities and options. The goal of providing universal access to key goods and services is often included in national development plans, national constitutions, and international agreements such as the Universal Declaration of Human Rights. This chapter presents a method to measure a society's progress as it moves toward attaining universal access.

At first glance, one might think that simply measuring coverage rates suffices. But this has a fundamental shortcoming. As a country develops, the opportunity to access key goods and services is only partial; they are scarce and can be allocated in many different ways. The allocation of goods and services within the population is never random and in many cases is not egalitarian. An equitable development process should seek to ensure that the opportunity for children to access these key goods and services is not correlated with circumstances that are beyond their control, such as gender, parental background, or ethnicity. The Human Opportunity Index (HOI), first presented by Barros and others (2009), combines both coverage rates and equity in a single measure. The HOI considers (1) how far a country is from the goal of providing universal access to a set of goods and services to all and (2) the degree to which each child in the country has an equal opportunity to access those good and services.

Equality of opportunity requires that access to key goods and services not be related to variables we call *circumstances*. Circumstances are personal, family, or community characteristics that a child has no control over and that, for ethical reasons, society wants to be completely unrelated to a child's access to basic opportunities. For instance, most societies would agree that opportunities should not be assigned based on gender, ethnicity, nationality, parental background, or religion. Instead, opportunities should be allocated nonsystematically and not be detrimental to any particular social group. The HOI measures the coverage rate and then adjusts it according to how equitably goods and services have been allocated among circumstance groups.

This chapter discusses what characterizes basic goods and services and the implications of allocating them equitably. We also present the conceptual underpinnings of the HOI. It is a synthetic measure of how far a society is from universal access to a good or service, and how equitably access is distributed across circumstance groups. We briefly outline the HOI's properties and present decompositions illustrating how progress can be made by expanding average coverage and/or more equitably distributing opportunities of access. Last, we outline a methodology to operationalize these concepts in 19 Latin American and Caribbean countries to assess progress during the last decade in universalizing basic opportunities for children. The empirical results are presented in the following chapter.

Key Concepts: Basic Goods and Services, Universality, Equality of Opportunity and Circumstances

Having opportunities means that people can pursue the life of their choosing. A critical aspect of this is having access to key goods and services that are fundamentally important for a person to lead a dignified life in modern society. Access gives a person the *opportunity* to advance, although they may or may not ultimately achieve this advancement. In some cases, having access to one specific good or service is not enough.

For example, the opportunity to learn requires a bundle of goods and services—access to a good school might not be enough; a child also needs adequate nutrition to have the opportunity to learn.

The HOI focuses on goods and services that constitute investments by people in themselves—those that improve a person's ability to expand her future production possibility frontier. These investments have a major impact on what a person can be or do, affecting both market and nonmarket outcomes. In this broad sense, investing in these goods and services increases one's *human capital.*

Our attention is limited to private goods and services that expand people's chances of living a better life. They are private in the traditional economic sense of being excludable. As long as the provision of these goods and services entails a cost and there are finite resources (i.e., a budget constraint), allocative decisions are required. Given the paramount importance of allocative decisions to economic and social policy, this study focuses precisely on access to goods or services that expand chances, and not on other dimensions of policy that might also play that role.[1]

Basic Goods and Services and Universality

Societies may decide that the universal access to selected goods and services should be a major social goal. Goals of this sort are often elucidated in national development plans and sometimes national constitutions; they are also laid out in the Universal Declaration of Human Rights. Whenever a national consensus exists that some goods and services should be enjoyed by everyone, we refer to them as *basic.* Even though the set of basic goods and services may vary with the socioeconomic and cultural context, the top priorities seem to be quite similar among all societies. To be considered basic, goods and services also need to be affordable— otherwise universal access would not be economically feasible.

A societal goal of universal access does not necessarily imply either how universality is to be accomplished or who is responsible. Even if universal access to a basic good or service is defined as a social right, it does not automatically mean that the *public* sector is responsible for provision or financing. In the extreme, a society may set a goal of universal access even when the responsibility is entirely individual, not collective. For instance, to set a goal of universal access to adequate nutrition does not necessarily imply that everyone is entitled to receive a monthly food basket from the government. Societies may use multiple mechanisms to achieve universality. Universal access to primary education may be ensured through a system of free public schools, through a privately managed but publicly funded system, through a public school system that recovers costs from wealthier families only, or through private schools with partial or full scholarships depending on family resources.

Assessing Progress toward Opportunity for All: Limitation of the Coverage Rate as a Measure

If universal access to basic goods and services is to be considered a major development goal, then it is critical to develop adequate measures of the progress toward its accomplishment. Traditionally, the coverage rate—the proportion of the population with access to a given opportunity—has been used to measure progress. It certainly seems natural to measure progress by the distance of the coverage rate to its ideal 100 percent. However, measures of progress should be sensitive to allocation. When societies have sufficient resources to provide something to everybody, there will be no allocation dilemma. However, when available resources allow only for providing key goods and services to some, the decision of who enjoys access depends on allocation. In this situation, measures of progress toward the ideal of opportunity for all should privilege egalitarian allocation.

Consider, for instance, two societies (I and II) comprising two ethnic groups (A and B) of equal population size. Suppose that, at the current time, enough resources are at hand to give access to a specific service only to half of the population. Hence, in both societies the average coverage rate is 50 percent. Suppose, however, that in Society I the service is allocated to ethnic group A and not at all to group B—the coverage rates are 100 percent for group A and 0 percent for group B. By contrast, in Society II both ethnic groups equally share the limited available services, and as a consequence the coverage rate is 50 percent in both groups. Hence, even though both societies have the same average coverage rate, they differ remarkably in the allocation of their scarce services. In principle, the allocation rules of Society II are more egalitarian. As a consequence, any valid measure ought to indicate that Society II is closer than Society I to the ideal of equitably allocating goods and services, even if the total coverage rate in both is only 50 percent. A single aggregated coverage rate is not enough to track progress toward the ideal of opportunity to all because it is insensitive to the fairness of allocation.

Equality of Opportunity, Circumstances, and Incidence Analysis

This report, in the tradition of the *World Development Report 2006: Equity and Development* and of Barros and others (2009), adopts a notion of fairness that is related to equality of opportunities. To the extent that basic goods and service are scarce and indivisible, some people will have access to them and others will not. According to the principle of equality of opportunity, everybody should have the same chance of accessing them, regardless of their circumstances. In the example of two societies presented above, incidence analysis—which breaks down coverage by different socioeconomic and demographic groups—uncovers differences in coverage rates for each ethnic group. For equality of opportunity to prevail, all group-specific coverage rates must be the same.

Circumstances, as used here, are personal, family, or community characteristics over which an individual has no direct control. For ethical reasons, society wants these to be completely unrelated (directly or indirectly) to one's access to basic opportunities. Boys and girls should all have the same opportunities to access good quality education and adequate nutrition, irrespective of the education of their parents, their ethnicity, or their place of birth. That is, when basic opportunities are limited, they should be allocated nonsystematically and in a way not detrimental to any particular group.

The ethical ideal of equal opportunity is intimately related to equal treatment, lack of discrimination, citizenship, and personal development independent of socioeconomic origin. What exactly determines which characteristics are considered a circumstance is more complex. One provides either an exhaustive list of all circumstances or a general rule for identifying whether a characteristic is a circumstance. Any set of circumstances as used here is subjective or at least relative. Ultimately, each society chooses its own set of circumstances that it believes should not interfere with access to basic goods and services.

In some cases, circumstances may have a role as policy instruments in the provision of goods and services because they are an efficient mechanism for expanding access. For example, despite the fact that a child should have access to basic nutrition regardless of their parent's income, social policy analysis might consider family income a valid instrument for children to obtain access to basic nutrition support programs. Thus, even though society *ideally* prefers that family income not be related to children's access to basic food, it may use income transfers as an instrument to reduce malnutrition on a transitional basis. Similarly, in the long run societies want all children to have access to adequate nutrition and health care independent of their mothers' education. However, because a mother's education has a critical role in providing more opportunities to get adequate nutrition and health care, social policies are in many cases designed to strengthen this externality.[2]

Incidence analysis is an improvement over a single aggregated coverage rate for measuring progress toward leveling the playing field because it can be sensitive to inequality of opportunity. Incidence analysis substitutes one coverage rate with many—one for each circumstance group. In the spirit of incidence analysis, one could say that, for equality of opportunity to prevail, all group-specific coverage rates must be the same. Incidence analysis, however, is not enough to measure progress toward opportunity for all because it does not provide a synthetic scalar *measure* of how far a society is from both equality of opportunity and universal coverage. To track hundreds of coverage rates would be too cumbersome to be useful to both policy makers and other key stakeholders in society.[3]

The scalar measure of equal opportunity progress toward universal access to basic goods and services, first presented in Barros and others (2009), takes into consideration both (a) average coverage and (b) if available goods or services are allocated equitably. A scalar measure of progress toward universality that combines these two features can be called an *equality of opportunity-sensitive coverage rate*.

Access, Utilization, Quality, and Outcomes

When measuring the access to specific goods and services, one must be very careful in defining what access means. Does access to schooling mean having a school nearby? Or having a good school nearby? Or attending school? Or having all the conditions needed to have a productive educational experience? Or achieving learning outcomes? One could easily imagine a situation in which a school or a health clinic exists in a community, but few actually take advantage of it. To the extent that opportunity is just the chance of accessing key goods and services for children, a strong argument is seen for universal coverage and defining equality of opportunity in terms of access and use.

For this study, we assume that as long as the focus of analysis is children, then access and utilization should be considered the same. A child may have access to a school reasonably close to his or her home but may not attend school because the parents do not value education or because the school is of very low quality. In this case, we treat the child as having no access to school. If this is a basic service, society must ensure that the child uses the service, which might entail not only having a school nearby but also maintaining schools at a level of quality sufficient to convince parents that it pays to send their children to school, educating parents on the benefits (economic and otherwise) of education, or enforcing attendance. Hence, we consider that coverage should be measured as a student enrolling and attending a formal school. Another consideration is quality. Basic goods and service are usually not homogeneous, and quality might vary tremendously. If, for example, clean water is a basic good or service, it is important to empirically assess what modes of provision provide a minimum threshold of quality.

An alternative view considers coverage to extend only to those who benefit from the use and access of a basic good and service above a minimum threshold. It is *effective* access to services of *quality* that produce a minimum level of outcome. For instance, the best practical measure of effective access to quality education could be the proportion of children of a given age with learning proficiency above a minimum level. In this view, access is just a means to reach minimum levels of certain *outcomes* that ought to be compulsory.[4] It would not be sufficient to ensure universal access to schools of quality and to guarantee that all families have the conditions they need to fully take advantage of this opportunity. We do not pursue this alternative view because of the lack of comparable outcome indicators for all countries, as discussed below.

Constructing a Measure of Progress toward Basic Opportunities for All

In this section we introduce and evaluate the properties of the Human Opportunity Index (HOI), a synthetic scalar measure for monitoring both (a) the average coverage of a good or service and (b) if it is allocated according to an equality of opportunity principle.[5] Such scalar measures are fundamental for measuring progress toward the universal provision of basic goods and services. Such a summary measure could also be essential for improving targeting of neglected groups and for improving the effectiveness of a social policy aimed at universal access to basic goods and services.

The literature provides many measures of equality of opportunity, such as those presented in Barros, Molinas Vega, and Saavedra Chanduvi (2008), Bourguignon, Ferreira, and Menéndez (2007), Checchi and Peragine (2005), and Lefranc, Pistolesi, and Trannoy (2006), among others. The main contribution of this study is not only how to measure equality of opportunity, but also how to incorporate equality-of-opportunity concerns when evaluating coverage. As such, the HOI assesses the whole empirical distribution of the provision of opportunities to access a specific good or service. It encompasses both the average coverage rate of a basic good or service and a relative measure of equality of opportunity.

Constructing the Human Opportunity Index

Any equality of opportunity–sensitive coverage rate must take into account both the overall coverage and the differential coverage rates of the several circumstance groups that make up the whole population. The construction of an equality-sensitive coverage rate amounts to aggregating circumstance-specific rates in a scalar measure that, at the same time, increases with overall coverage and decreases with the differences in coverage among circumstance groups. One could imagine numerous alternative ways of constructing an equality of opportunity–sensitive coverage rate having these two properties. The HOI is based on discounting a penalty for inequality of opportunity P from the overall coverage rate C so that

$$HOI = C - P.$$

The penalty is chosen such that it is zero if all circumstance group-specific coverage rates are equal, and it is positive and increasing as differences in coverage among circumstance groups increase. This penalty makes the HOI sensitive to equality as well as overall coverage. Intuitively, P is larger the larger the dispersion of group-specific coverage rates. Only when the penalty is zero and average coverage is universal does the HOI reach the maximum value of one (see box 1.1 for computation details).

Below we present a graphical explanation of the computation and interpretation of the HOI. The explanation uses data on access to safe water for 16-year-old children in a fictitious country (a detailed numerical example can be found in annex A1.1). In the first example, the overall average coverage rate is 59 percent, and each circumstance group-specific coverage rate is also 59 percent, meaning this is a situation of equality of opportunity (figure 1.1). The average coverage rate line represents the equal opportunity line. Even though access is not related to circumstances, the playing field is not level because 41 percent of the children do not have access to safe water, whereas 59 percent do.

In the second situation, 59 percent of children still have access to safe water and 41 percent do not, but now the allocation is related to children's circumstances, and as such there is no equality of opportunity (figure 1.2).[6] Those circumstance groups with coverage rates below the overall average rate are called "opportunity vulnerable" groups.

To calculate the HOI for the second situation, the penalty refers to access to safe water that was allocated in violation of the equal opportunity

Box 1.1

Computing the Penalty for Inequality of Opportunity

Computing P requires identifying all circumstance groups with coverage rates below the average rate; we refer to them as the opportunity-vulnerable groups. For each opportunity-vulnerable group k, $\bar{M}_k$ *is the number of people with access to a good or service needed* for its coverage rate to equal the average rate, and M_k is the number of people in group k, with access. $M_k - \bar{M}_k$ is then the opportunity gap for the vulnerable group k. The penalty is the sum of the opportunity gaps of all vulnerable groups (called the overall opportunity gap) divided by the total population (N):

$$P = \frac{1}{N}\sum_{k=1}^{v}\left(M_k - \bar{M}_k\right).$$

Intuitively, P can be interpreted as the percentage of people whose access would have to be reassigned to people in the groups with below-average coverage rates to achieve equality of opportunity. If all groups had exactly the same coverage rate, that penalty would be zero, and no reassignment would be needed. As coverage approaches universality for all groups, that reassignment becomes smaller.

principle (figure 1.3). Every allocation of access to water to circumstances groups above the overall average is a violation of the equality-of-opportunity principle, because access to safe water is not independent of circumstances. In this example, 10 percent of access to water was allocated inequitably. The HOI is equal to the average coverage rate (59 percent) minus the penalty for inequality of opportunity (10 percent): 49 percent. In other words, the HOI can be thought of as the weighted average of the circumstance group-specific coverage rates for all groups with below-average coverage.

Properties

This section discusses three important properties of the HOI. First, it is defined as an equality-sensitive coverage rate. As such, its value falls as inequality in the allocation of a given fixed number of opportunities increases. In this case, the opportunity gap may increase (it will never decrease), leading to a corresponding increase in the penalty.

Second, this equality-sensitive measure is Pareto consistent. In principle, sensitivity to equality should never be so large that the index would

Figure 1.1 Percentage of 16-Year-Olds with Access to Safe Water: Equal Opportunity Allocation

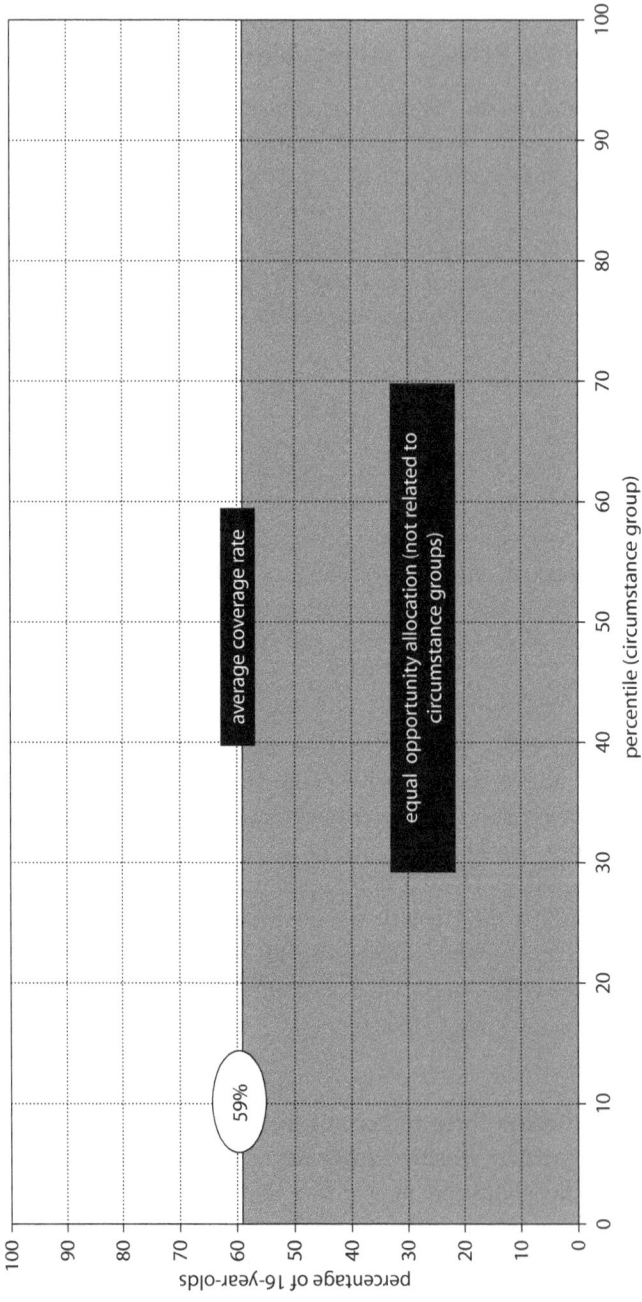

average coverage rate

59%

equal opportunity allocation (not related to circumstance groups)

percentage of 16-year-olds

percentile (circumstance group)

Source: Authors' simulations for a fictitious country.

Figure 1.2 Percentage of 16-Year-Olds with Access to Safe Water: Unequal Opportunity Allocation

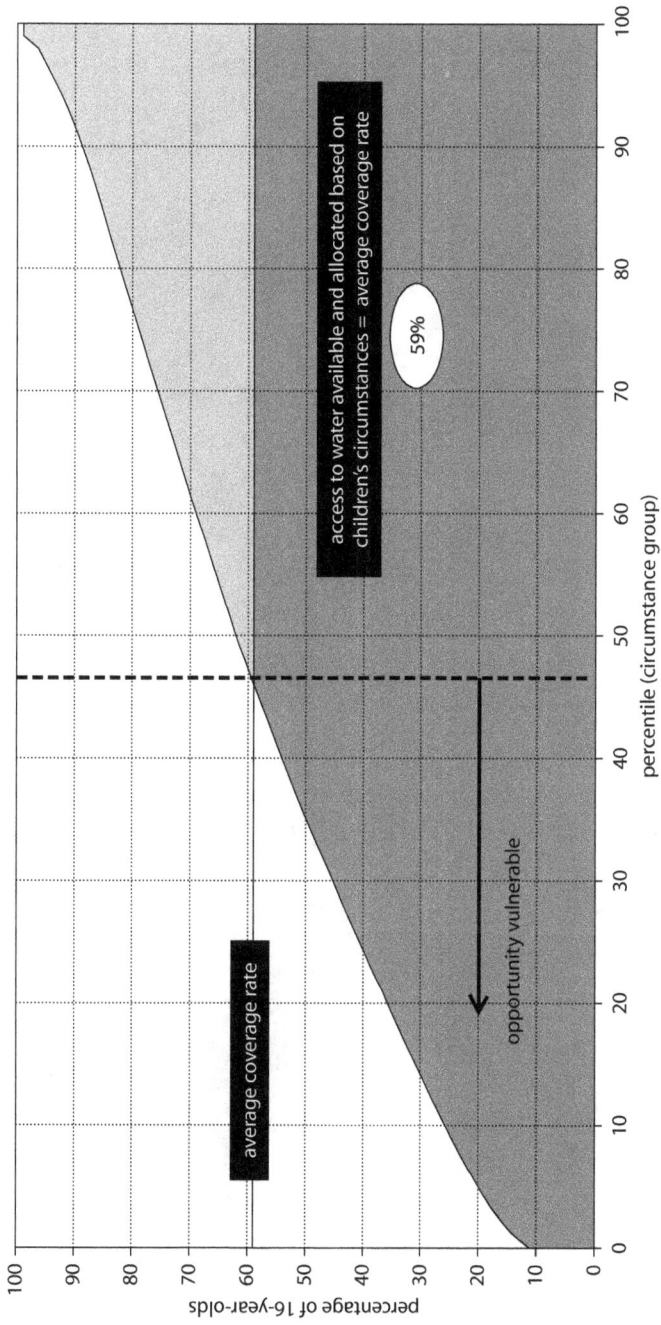

Source: Authors' simulations for a fictitious country.

Figure 1.3   Penalty for Inequality of Opportunity and the Human Opportunity Index

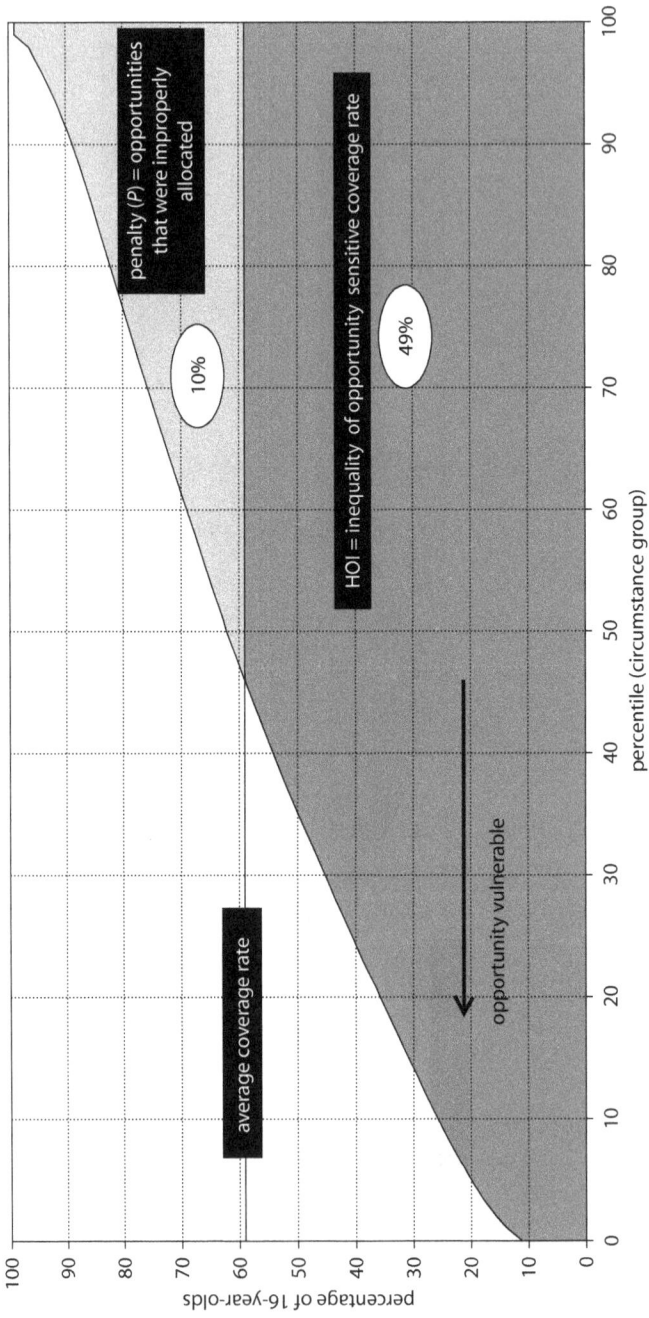

Legend within figure:
- penalty (P) = opportunities that were improperly allocated — 10%
- HOI = inequality of opportunity sensitive coverage rate — 49%
- average coverage rate
- opportunity vulnerable
- percentage of 16-year-olds
- percentile (circumstance group)

Source: Authors' simulations for a fictitious country.

decline when no one loses access but someone that previously had no access gains access. Even though inequality may increase sharply, no coverage rate for any circumstance group would decline. Hence, there is no reason for the overall score to worsen. The HOI is indeed Pareto consistent. Whenever no one loses access and at least someone gains access, the index will always improve, regardless of whether that person belongs to an opportunity-vulnerable group or not.

Third, when the coverage rates of all circumstance groups increase proportionally, the HOI will increase by the same proportion. It can be easily established that in this case both the coverage and the penalty would also increase by the same percentage, as would the index. In the case of an equal increase in percentage points for all group-specific coverage rates, the index would also increase by the same percentage points. In this case, all differences in coverage rates and the penalty would remain unchanged, whereas the overall coverage—and hence the index—would increase by the same percentage points.

Thus, when (a) inequality declines and overall coverage remains constant or (b) overall coverage increases while inequality remains constant, the HOI will always improve. So it is, in fact, a valid inequality-sensitive coverage rate. Last, because the HOI is equal to the difference between the overall coverage rate and the penalty, it is always equal to or lower than the coverage rate. The coverage rate is lower than one (that is, less than 100 percent), and so too is the index.

The HOI and the Dissimilarity Index

Using a penalty allows us to define an equality-sensitive coverage rate without actually measuring the level of inequality of opportunities. But a measure of relative inequality in the allocation of the opportunities D could be easily obtained by dividing the penalty P by the overall coverage rate C. This measure might be constructed as a "Dissimilarity Index" to measure dissimilar coverage rates across groups defined by circumstances. This index stands for the fraction of people who would need to have a good or service reassigned as a percentage of all people who have access to the good or service. Accordingly, $(1 - D)$ would stand for the percentage of available opportunities that were properly allocated. It can be shown that

$$\text{HOI} = C - P = C \times (1 - D).$$

Hence, the HOI can be seen as the average coverage rate, discounted by one minus the inequality index D. An alternative interpretation of the

Dissimilarity Index is that it is proportional to the difference between group-specific coverage rates and average coverage rates. The larger the difference, the larger is D. If all group-specific coverage rates are equal to the average, $D = 0$, and the HOI is equal to the overall average coverage rate (C).

Decomposing Changes in the HOI: Composition and Coverage Effects

The HOI is determined by group-specific coverage rates and their corresponding population shares (the distribution of circumstances).[7] As a result, the HOI can change only when at least one of these two features changes. Hence, any change in the index can be traced either to changes in the distribution of circumstances (*composition effect*) or to changes in at least some group-specific coverage rates (*coverage effect*). The coverage effect can be further decomposed into changes because of changes in equality of opportunity (*equalization effect*) and changes because of average coverage rates (*scale effect*). Below we discuss the intuition behind each effect. A numerical example and the algebra of the decompositions are found in annexes A1.2 and A1.3.

The composition effect. Even though any change in the HOI can always be decomposed into composition and coverage effects, these two components do not have the same importance. The HOI measures progress toward the goal of opportunities for all. What matters is how far group-specific coverage rates are from the ideal of 100 percent. The distribution of circumstances is used only to weight the remaining gaps. If equality of opportunity prevails and all group-specific coverage rates are equal, changes in the distribution of circumstances will have no effect on the HOI. Once all group-specific coverage rates reach 100 percent, the goal will be reached irrespective of the distribution of circumstance.

Nevertheless, although inequality of opportunity remains large, changes in the HOI could still come from changes in the distribution of circumstances, known as the *composition effect*. Most of the composition effect reflects structural demographic changes, overall economic development, and increased investments in education. In certain cases, reducing the share in the population of certain groups could be, at least temporarily, an effective instrument to progress toward universal coverage. For instance, if malnutrition rates among children from income-poor families are hard to reduce, an alternative policy could be to decrease the proportion of children in poor families through income transfers.

The coverage effect: Scale and equalization. Progress in coverage can be achieved in two very distinct ways. One would be to increase all group-specific coverage rates proportionally. In this case, the degree of equality of opportunity would remain unchanged, and the HOI would increase exclusively because of a change in the average coverage rate. We call this type of change a *scale effect*.

On the other hand, progress could be achieved by increasing coverage rates among vulnerable groups, compensated by a concomitant decrease in coverage rates among nonvulnerable groups that would hold the overall coverage rate unchanged. In this case because the overall rate remains unchanged, the HOI increases only because of the decline in the degree of inequality of opportunity. We call this type of change an *equalization effect*.

All changes in coverage can be expressed as a combination of a scale and an equalization effect. Hence, in principle the coverage effect can always be further decomposed into a scale and an equalization effect.

Empirical Considerations for Constructing the Human Opportunity Index

The HOI is constructed in three steps. First, we must select a specific basic good or service to focus on and define minimum standards to fully characterize access. Second, we must choose a set of relevant circumstances. Third, based on microdata from household surveys, we compute the coverage rate and the penalty for the specific basic good or service at hand.

Basic Goods and Services Considered and Minimum Standards

The HOI focuses on access to key goods and services by children 16 years of age and under. Independent of the intrinsic value of measuring access to key goods and services by children, focusing on this age range obviates the need to make any distinction between access and utilization related to effort, attitudes, or preferences of the child or parents. The assumption is that as long as society agrees on universalizing an opportunity, it must ensure utilization by children independently of the preferences of the child or his or her family.

In principle, a set of the most basic goods and services for children is quite large, covering a wide range of what is needed for children to develop themselves and pursue a life of their choice. To make cross-country comparisons, we need comparable information on basic goods and services for all countries considered. The challenge stems from different survey terminologies and sometimes different national standards regarding adequate levels of service. For instance, access to safe water must have the same meaning and be measured similarly in all countries. To ensure comparability across countries and over time, a set of five indicators was chosen to represent the dimensions of education and housing (see annex A1.4 for more details on the indicators):

- *Education dimension.* To capture the effective opportunity to quality education we use *completion of sixth grade at the proper age* (13 years old). Children completing sixth grade on time are more likely to have had access to schools of reasonable quality that ensure minimum learning and consequently can avoid unnecessary grade repetition. Some education systems in the region, however, adopt automatic promotion whereas others do not, leading to potential intercountry comparability problems. To balance the potential comparability due to automatic promotions, we include *school attendance of children 10 to 14 years old* as an additional indicator.

- *Housing dimension.* To evaluate the opportunity to an enhanced quality of life we use the access to basic housing services: *safe water, adequate sanitation,* and *electricity.*

  a. *Access to safe water and adequate sanitation.* Water and sanitation are primary drivers of public health. A vast literature finds a strong negative relationship between children's mortality rates and improved water sources and sanitation facilities (for example, Abou-Ali Hala 2003; Fuentes, Pfütze, and Seck 2006; Galiani, Gertler, and Schargrodsky 2005; Rutstein 2000). Improved water and sanitation are linked to reduced incidence of diarrhea and related serious long-term consequences such as malnutrition, opportunistic infections (such as pneumonia), and physical or mental stunting. Moreover, WHO estimates that every year 1.4 million children under the age of five die from diarrheal diseases attributed to unsafe water supply and inadequate sanitation and hygiene (WHO 2002).

  b. *Access to electricity.* Electricity enhances the quality of life in numerous ways. First, it can promote a healthier lifestyle, for instance, by improving air quality as electric stoves replace indoor biomass cook stoves. This is particularly helpful for young children and mothers. Replacing kerosene lamps with electricity has also been shown to reduce eye irritation, coughing, and nasal problems and to reduce the substantial number of children who die annually from accidental kerosene poisoning (Kaufman and others 2000). But perhaps more important, other opportunities are opened by access to electricity: improved conditions for studying in the evenings; accessing information and entertainment via radio, television, and the Internet; freeing parents' time from domestic chores so they could potentially spend that time raising their children; and home and community safety. Studies have documented that children spend more time studying after electricity is provided (Gustavsson 2007), and electricity allows access to modern educational techniques using computers, as in rural Peru (Bajak 2007).

To ensure intercountry comparability we opt to use the simplest possible concept for adequate access to water, sanitation, and electricity. Most surveys in the region do not ask directly about potable (safe) water, but about the location and type of the water source and the system used for distribution. As a result, we consider as having access all households with water from the public network inside the dwelling. For sanitation, we consider as having access all households that have flush toilets inside the property that are connected to a waste removal system. For electricity, we consider access from any source adequate.

The basic goods and services used in this study all vary extensively in quality. It is clear that, for example, access to schooling hides a large variance in the quality of the service, whereas frequent blackouts, rationing, and diminished wattage hinder the benefits a family can draw from access to electricity. Data access and comparability limitations make it difficult to gauge quality in basic goods and services. At this stage, for comparability purposes, the analysis is limited to indicators that measure quantity and not quality. Further analysis at the country level should incorporate the quality dimension, both because quality of services is a critical area of improvement in all countries, and also because large inequalities of quality of services are found across different groups of the population.

Choosing Circumstances

By circumstances we mean personal, family, or community characteristics that a society believes should not play a role in determining access to basic opportunities. For instance, most societies would agree that opportunities to access key goods and services should not be based on gender, ethnicity, nationality, parental background, or religion. To the extent that equal opportunity requires independence from socioeconomic origin, parents' education and family income should also be treated as circumstances. Location of residence (urban versus rural) may also be considered a circumstance, to the extent that a society believes that all children should have equal access to the same opportunities independently of where they live. This wide scope of circumstances represents a major challenge to any empirical work because of data limitations.

Moreover, to assess the relative performance of different countries requires a set of empirically tractable circumstances and basic goods and services. Unfortunately, such a set—available for all countries—is limited. Instead, we must use information collected with reasonably similar methods across countries. For instance, if we wish to use family income as a circumstance, we must construct compatible income aggregates for all countries. However, important circumstances, such as ethnicity, have distinct categories in different contexts, so they are trickier to use in regional studies. Although in Brazil, Colombia, and Panama the distinction between African and European descendants may be of major importance, in Bolivia and Guatemala the most important distinction may be between indigenous people and European descendants. This type of variable is therefore difficult to use in a study that compares a set of countries.

For this study, to ensure comparability across countries and over time, a set of seven circumstances was chosen:

1. Parents' education (to capture socioeconomic origin)
2. Family per capita income (to capture availability of resources)
3. Number of siblings (to capture the dependency ratio)
4. The presence of both parents (to capture family structure)
5. Gender of the child (to capture one direct form of discrimination)
6. Gender of the household head (to capture one indirect form of discrimination)
7. Urban or rural location of residence (to capture spatial disparities)

Computing the Human Opportunity Index for Access to a Basic Good or Service

Given a random sample of the population, with information on whether child i had access to a given basic good or service and a vector of variables indicating his or her circumstances, we first use a regression model to estimate the empirical relationship between each circumstance and access to basic service. We then are able to predict the probability of access to a basic service for each individual with a given set of circumstances as well as the overall coverage rate. The next step is the core of the concept of inequality of opportunity, as we seek to derive an overall estimate of the extent of the variation in the coverage rates of individual children in the target population compared with the average coverage. The greater the variation, the higher the inequality of opportunity and the smaller the HOI (box 1.2).

Box 1.2

The Six Steps of Building the Human Opportunity Index

1. Estimate a separable logistic model on whether child i had access to a given basic good or service as a function of his or her circumstances. For education, age was also used to predict the probability of completing each grade. The specification was chosen according to the needs of each circumstance: quadratic for years of education, logarithmic for real income, and categorical for age and the other dimensions. In all cases the functions are linear in the parameters. From the estimation of this logistic regression, obtain coefficient estimates.

2. Given these coefficient estimates, obtain for each child in the sample the predicted probability of access to the basic good or service in consideration $\hat{p}_i$ based on the predicted relationship $\hat{\beta}_k$ and a vector of their circumstances x_{ki}:

$$\hat{p}_i = \frac{\exp\left(\hat{\beta}_o + \sum_{k=1}^{m} x_{ki}\hat{\beta}_k\right)}{1+\exp\left(\hat{\beta}_o + \sum_{k=1}^{m} x_{ki}\hat{\beta}_k\right)}.$$

3. Compute the overall coverage rate C,

$$C = \sum_{1}^{n} w_i \hat{p}_i,$$

where $w_i = \frac{1}{n}$ or some sampling weights.

4. Compute the Dissimilarity Index $\hat{D}$,

$$\hat{D} = \frac{1}{2C} \sum_{i=1}^{n} w_i |\hat{p}_i - C|.$$

5. Compute the penalty, $P = C \times \hat{D}$.
6. Compute the HOI $= C - P$.

Constructing an Overall Human Opportunity Index

To generate a single measure of the distribution of opportunities for children, we need to construct an overall synthetic HOI comprising all basic goods and services under consideration. The overall HOI, in this study, is a simple average of the HOI of the two dimensions considered: education and housing. The HOI for education is a simple average of the HOI for completion of sixth grade on time and the HOI for school attendance for children 10–14 years old. The HOI for housing is a simple average of the HOI for access to water, the HOI for sanitation, and the HOI for electricity.[8]

The next chapter presents the empirical results for the HOI for the Latin America and the Caribbean region. It tracks the changes children have faced in accessing opportunities for education and housing services in the region between 1995 and 2010 and decomposes the contributions of the composition and coverage effects. It also presents a snapshot of how circumstances have affected inequality of opportunity for the region's children in the last 15 years.

Annex A1.1. A Numerical Example of Computing the HOI

To help explain the computation of the HOI, we use the example presented in tables A1.1a–i, in which the overall population is divided in 16 circumstance groups, defined by gender, race, and location. We assume that all groups are the same size: 100 persons, leading to a total population of 1,600. Table A1.1a presents the number of people in each circumstance group that have access to a specific basic service (for example, clean water, electricity, or vaccinations). Overall, 400 people have access to the service. Because the total population is 1,600, the overall coverage rate is 25 percent. Under equality of opportunity, 25 percent of each circumstance group should be covered. Coverage

Table A1.1a   Distribution of a Service

		North		South	
		Urban	Rural	Urban	Rural
Men	Whites	75	60	45	20
	Blacks	50	50	30	20
Women	Whites	15	10	5	0
	Blacks	15	5	0	0

Source: Authors' calculations.
Note: Units are counts.

Table A1.1b   Group-Specific Coverage Rates

		North		South	
		Urban	Rural	Urban	Rural
Men	Whites	75%	60%	45%	20%
	Blacks	50%	50%	30%	20%
Women	Whites	15%	10%	5%	0%
	Blacks	15%	5%	0%	0%

Source: Authors' calculations.
Note: Units are counts.

Table A1.1c   Opportunity Gaps (for Vulnerable Groups)

		North		South	
		Urban	Rural	Urban	Rural
Men	Whites	0	0	0	5
	Blacks	0	0	0	5
Women	Whites	10	15	20	25
	Blacks	10	20	25	25

Source: Authors' calculations.
Note: Units are counts.

Table A1.1d   Distribution of the Population

		North		South	
		Urban	Rural	Urban	Rural
Men	Whites	100	100	100	100
	Blacks	100	100	100	100
Women	Whites	100	100	100	100
	Blacks	100	100	100	100

Source: Authors' calculations.
Note: Units are counts.

Table A1.1e   Opportunity Gaps as a Proportion of the Total Population

		North		South	
		Urban	Rural	Urban	Rural
Men	Whites	0%	0%	0%	0%
	Blacks	0%	0%	0%	0%
Women	Whites	1%	1%	1%	2%
	Blacks	1%	1%	2%	2%

Source: Authors' calculations.
Note: Units are counts.

Table A1.1f   Opportunity Gaps as a Proportion of the Population Covered

		North		South	
		Urban	Rural	Urban	Rural
Men	Whites	0%	0%	0%	1%
	Blacks	0%	0%	0%	1%
Women	Whites	3%	4%	5%	6%
	Blacks	3%	5%	6%	6%

Source: Authors' calculations.
Note: Units are counts.

Table A1.1g   Improperly Allocated Services

		North		South	
		Urban	Rural	Urban	Rural
Men	Whites	50	35	20	0
	Blacks	25	25	5	0
Women	Whites	0	0	0	0
	Blacks	0	0	0	0

Source: Authors' calculations.
Note: Units are counts.

Table A1.1h   Improperly Allocated Services as a Proportion of the Total Population

		North		South	
		Urban	Rural	Urban	Rural
Men	Whites	3%	2%	1%	0%
	Blacks	2%	2%	0%	0%
Women	Whites	0%	0%	0%	0%
	Blacks	0%	0%	0%	0%

Source: Authors' calculations.
Note: Units are counts.

Table A1.1i   Improperly Allocated Services as a Proportion of the Population Covered

		North		South	
		Urban	Rural	Urban	Rural
Men	Whites	13%	9%	5%	0%
	Blacks	6%	6%	1%	0%
Women	Whites	0%	0%	0%	0%
	Blacks	0%	0%	0%	0%

Source: Authors' calculations.
Note: Units are counts.

rates, however, vary substantially, from 0 percent in some groups to 75 percent in others (table A1.1b).

The computation of the penalty is done in three steps. First, we identify all circumstance groups with a coverage rate below the average rate (25 percent in our example); we refer to them as the opportunity-vulnerable groups. There are 10 such groups in our example, shaded gray in table A1.1b. Second, we compute the gap between the number of people in each vulnerable group that should have access to the service for the group to reach the average coverage rate and the actual number of people with access to the service in that group (table A1.1c).

Third, the penalty is obtained by dividing the sum of the opportunity gaps of all vulnerable groups (called the overall opportunity gap) by the total population. In our example, the penalty would be equal to 10 percent, because the sum of all opportunity gaps equals 160 (table A1.1c), and the overall population is 1,600. The overall coverage rate of 25 percent minus the penalty due to unequal allocation of 10 percent leads to an HOI of 15 percent ($C - P = $ HOI; $25 - 10 = 15$).

In this example, only 90 individuals from opportunity-vulnerable groups are covered, out of 250 that should have been covered had equality of opportunity prevailed. Hence, 160 people among these vulnerable groups should receive the service for their coverage rate to rise at least to the average. This total opportunity gap, 160, equals 10 percent of the total population.

Because services are available for 400 people, and 160 people in non–opportunity-vulnerable groups receive services in excess of what is needed for equality of opportunity to prevail, only 240 people received services that were allocated equitably. Hence, as a proportion of the total population, the number of people who receive the service according to the principle of equality of opportunities is 15 percent (240/1,600). *This is what the HOI measures.*

Annex A1.2. Numerical Illustration of the Decomposition of the HOI

The HOI can be easily computed from the distribution of the population by circumstance groups (table A1.2.1a) and specific coverage rates (table A1.2.1b) through four simple steps (table A1.2.1c). First, we compute the overall coverage rate as the weighted average of all group-specific coverage rates (35 percent in population A). Second, we identify groups with specific coverage rates below average (shaded gray). Third, we obtain the penalty (12.5 percent in population A) by weighting the difference between the overall coverage and each group-specific coverage rate among vulnerable groups: $(35 - 15) \times 0.25 + (35 - 5) \times 0.25 = 12.5$. Finally, we obtain the HOI (22.5 percent in population A) by subtracting the penalty from the overall coverage.

Using the same procedure and the information for population B in the last row of table A1.2.4c, we obtain an HOI of 37 percent for population B. One can think of populations A and B as being the same country in two different time periods. Population B has an HOI 14.5 percentage points higher than that of population A. This difference is due to disparities in both the distribution of the populations among circumstance groups and the pattern of their specific coverage rates. In population B, the north region has a 20 percentage point (p.p.) higher population share. In terms of coverage rates, those among the vulnerable groups tend to be higher in population B, whereas those among the non-vulnerable groups are higher in population A. Coverage rates are on average higher and less unequal in population B than in population A.

To isolate the effect on the HOI of differences in the distribution of population among circumstance groups, we estimate the HOI for a combined situation: Coverage rates are still those of population A, but

Table A1.2.1a   Distribution of Population A

100%	North	South
Men	25%	25%
Women	25%	25%

Source: Authors' calculations.

Table A1.2.1b   Group-Specific Coverage Rates for Population A

35%	North	South
Men	75%	45%
Women	15%	5%

Source: Authors' calculations.

Table A1.2.1c   Computing the HOI for Population A

Overall coverage rate	35.0%
Penalty	12.5%
HOI	22.5%

Source: Authors' calculations.

Table A1.2.2a   Distribution of Population B

35%	North	South
Men	40%	10%
Women	30%	20%

Source: Authors' calculations.

Table A1.2.2b   Group-Specific Coverage Rates for Population A

40%	North	South
Men	75%	45%
Women	15%	5%

Source: Authors' calculations.

Table A1.2.2c   Computing the HOI for Population B with the Coverage Rates from Population A

Overall coverage rate	40.0%
Penalty	14.5%
HOI	25.5%

Source: Authors' calculations.

the distribution of the population among circumstance groups is now that of population B. The estimated HOI for this hybrid situation is 25.5 percent.

Because this hybrid population shares with population A the same group-specific coverage rate, their difference in HOI (3.0 p.p.) is entirely due to their differences in the distribution of the population among circumstance groups. This is the *composition effect*. On the other hand, because the hybrid population shares with population B the same distribution of the population among circumstance groups, their difference in HOI (11.5 p.p.) is entirely due to their differences in their specific coverage rates. Hence, this difference is the *coverage effect*. Hence, the total difference in HOI (14.5 p.p.) between populations A and B is decomposed into the composition effect of 3 p.p. and 11.5 p.p. because of the coverage effect.

The coverage effect can be decomposed further (tables A1.2.3a–c). The group-specific coverage rates in table A1.2.3b are constructed to reach the average level in population B, holding the inequality level of population A. This is accomplished by proportionally increasing all group-specific rates from population A. Inequality would be preserved while the average coverage rate is adjusted. To reach the average coverage rate of population B, all group-specific coverage rates from population A are multiplied by the ratio between the overall coverage for populations B and A (45/40 = 1.125).[9]

As a consequence, the HOIs in tables A1.2.3c and A1.2.4c share the same distribution of the population among circumstance groups and the same overall coverage rate (45 percent). They differ only with respect to the inequality of their group-specific coverage rates. Since the overall coverage rate is the same in both cases, the difference in inequality is captured by corresponding differences in the size of the penalty: 16.3 percent in table A1.2.3c and 8 percent in table A1.2.4c. The difference between these two penalties, 8.3 p.p., is a measure of the *equalization effect*. It is the contribution of the greater equality of opportunities in population B to the difference in HOI between the two populations.

On the other hand, tables A1.2.2c and A1.2.3c share the same distribution of the population and the same inequality among group-specific coverage rates as measured by the ratio between the penalty and the overall coverage rate. This ratio is equal to 0.3625 in the two cases. Hence, the difference between HOIs in these tables (3.2 p.p.) is entirely due to their corresponding differences in overall coverage rates. It represents the *scale effect*.

Table A1.2.3a   Distribution of Population B

100%	North	South
Men	40%	10%
Women	30%	20%

Source: Authors' calculations.

Table A1.2.3b   Group-Specific Coverage Rates (Structure from Population A, Average Level from Population B)

45%	North	South
Men	84%	51%
Women	17%	6%

Source: Authors' calculations.

Table A1.2.3c   Computing the HOI for Population B with the Structure of Coverage Rates from Population A and Average Level from Population B

Overall coverage rate	45.0%
Penalty	16.3%
HOI	28.7%

Source: Authors' calculations.

Table A1.2.4a   Distribution of Population B

100%	North	South
Men	40%	10%
Women	30%	20%

Source: Authors' calculations.

Table A1.2.4b   Group-Specific Coverage Rates for Population B

45%	North	South
Men	65%	40%
Women	40%	15%

Source: Authors' calculations.

Table A1.2.4c   Computing the HOI for Population B

Overall coverage rate	45.0%
Penalty	8.0%
HOI	37.0%

Source: Authors' calculations.

Annex A1.3. The Algebra of Decomposing the Human Opportunity Index

Consider two populations, A and B. Let w_k^A denote the population share of circumstance-group k, and C_k^A is its specific coverage rate in population A, with w_k^B and C_k^B denoting the corresponding characteristics in population B. In this case, HOI^A can be expressed as

$$HOI^A = C^A - \sum_{k \in V^A} w_k^A \left(C^A - C_k^A \right),$$

where

$$C^A = \sum_k w_k^A C_k^A$$

and

$$V^A = \left\{ k : C_k^A < C^A \right\}$$

with similar expressions holding for HOI^B.

To obtain the decomposition, we begin with a hybrid HOI^{AB} combining the group-specific coverage rates of population A with the composition of population B:

$$HOI^{AB} = C^{AB} - \sum_{k \in V^{AB}} w_k^B \left(C^{AB} - C_k^A \right),$$

where

$$C^{AB} = \sum_k w_k^B C_k^A$$

and

$$V^{AB} = \left\{ k : C_k^A < C^{AB} \right\}.$$

Because HOI^A and HOI^{AB} share the same group-specific coverage rates, $\Delta = HOI^{AB} - HOI^A$ measures the composition effect, that is, the impact of differences in the distributions of the populations A and B among circumstance groups. On the other hand, because HOI^B and HOI^{AB} have the same population shares, $\Delta_r = HOI^B - HOI^{AB}$ measures the coverage effect, that is, the impact of the differences in group-specific coverage rates between populations A and B. Notice that the total difference is the sum of the coverage and composition effect: $\Delta = HOI^B - HOI^A = \Delta_r + \Delta_c$.

(continued next page)

To further decompose the coverage effect in an equalization effect and a scale effect, we construct the following hybrid group-specific coverage rate:

$$C_k^{AB} = C_k^A \frac{C^B}{C^{AB}}$$

Based on these hybrid group-specific coverage rates and noticing that

$$C^* = \sum_k w_k^B C_k^{AB} = C^B,$$

we estimate a new index via

$$HOI^* = C^B - \sum_{k \in V^*} w_k^B \left(C^B - C_k^{AB} \right),$$

where

$$V^* = \left\{ k : C_k^{AB} < C^B \right\}.$$

Because HOI^* and HOI^{AB} have the same population shares and level of inequality among group-specific coverage rates, $\Delta_s = HOI^* - HOI^{AB}$ measures the scale effect, that is, the impact of the differences in the level of the coverage rates between populations A and B. On the other hand, because HOI^B and HOI^* have the same population shares and overall coverage rate, $\Delta_e = HOI^B - HOI^*$ measures the equalization effect, that is, the impact of the differences in the degree of inequality among group-specific coverage rates between populations A and B. Notice that the coverage effect is the sum of the scale and equalization effects:

$$\Delta_r = HOI^B - HOI^{AB} = \Delta_s + \Delta_e$$

Annex A1.4. Indicators

Table A1.4   Definitions of Indicators

Indicator	Scope	Definition
Housing		
Adequate access to water	Children 0 to 16 years old	This variable takes the value of one if the household has access to running water within the dwelling. Thus, access includes public network connections and all water pumped into the dwelling, even if it is not from the public network.

(continued next page)

Table A1.4   *(continued)*

Indicator	Scope	Definition
Access to electricity	Children 0 to 16 years old	This variable takes the value of one if the dwelling has access to electricity from any source. Thus, sources can range from the electrical grid system to solar panels.
Adequate access to sanitation	Children 0 to 16 years old	This variable takes the value of one if the dwelling has access to a flush toilet (either inside the dwelling or inside the property) that is connected to any mechanism whereby household waste is allowed to flow away from the dwelling.
Education		
School attendance rate	Children 10 to 14 years old	This is measured as children aged 10–14 attending school, independent of grade. This variable measures the gross attendance rate.
Probability of completing sixth grade on time	Children 12 to 16 years old	This is measured by computing the probability of having ended sixth grade on time for all children ages 12 to 16. In most countries of the region, this means having completed primary education. Given that on average children start school at the age of 7, by age 13, students that have survived in the system without repetition should have completed six years of basic education.

Source: The World Bank and Universidad Nacional de La Plata (CEDLAS) Socioeconomic Database for Latin America and the Caribbean.

Annex A1.5. Choosing the Aggregation Sequence

To create an overall HOI, one needs to aggregate both the different dimensions of each person's opportunities (that is, the indicators used to proxy a basic opportunity) and the opportunities of different persons. Ideally, one should first aggregate the opportunities of each person, to fully consider the interdependence among the dimensions.

This interdependence among the dimensions has two features worth noting. First, the dimensions could be complements or substitutes. For instance, should attendance and progression in school be considered complements or substitutes? Second, the access to different goods and services could be concomitant or alternative. For instance, an overall 50 percent coverage rate for water and electricity could still lead to very distinct distributions. In one extreme, it may be the case that those having access to water are the same people having access to electricity. In this case, the accesses to these two services are perfectly correlated. On the other extreme, it may be that either one has access to water or to electricity, never to both. In this case, access to these two services is inversely related. If the two services are substitutes, an inverse relation is preferable. If they are complements, a positive association is preferable.

Hence, to properly evaluate opportunities one needs to know the degree of complementarity or substitutability between goods and services as well as the distribution of a population's access opportunities. Ultimately, aggregation takes into consideration the complementarities and substitutability among the many dimensions.

It may be useful to consider the extreme case in which the access opportunity is either 0 percent or 100 percent. Suppose I_1 indicates whether everyone has $(I_1 = 1)$ or does not have $(I_1 = 0)$ proper access to sanitation, and I_2 indicates whether everyone has $(I_2 = 1)$ or does not have $(I_2 = 0)$ adequate access to electricity. Three alternative aggregation strategies are possible in this example. The most demanding alternative would consider that one has an opportunity when he or she has access to both sanitation and electricity. In this case, the aggregated opportunity index would be $I = I_1 \times I_2$ and $I = 1$ if and only if $I_1 = 1$ and $I_2 = 1$. This is the *intersection approach*. In the other extreme, the least demanding alternative would consider the two opportunities as substitutes. In this case, having one of them is enough. Access to a second would not lead to any significant improvement. In this case, the aggregated opportunity index would be $I = 1 - (1 - I_1) \times (1 - I_2)$ and $I = 1$ if and only if $I_1 = 1$ *or* $I_2 = 1$. This is the *union approach*. An intermediate alternative is to relax the requirement that both are essential and, instead of going to the extreme that just one is enough, one may consider each one as an independent advantage. In this case, the aggregated opportunity index would be $I = I_1 + I_2$. This is the *counting approach*.

To properly take the distribution of access opportunity and degree of complementarity/substitutability into consideration, the many dimensions of opportunities faced by each person must be aggregated before aggregating among people. Once the aggregation across persons of each dimension is conducted, how positively or negatively correlated are the accesses to the many relevant key goods and services is lost.

A comprehensive consideration of the interrelation among dimensions also demands that information on the many dimensions be available for each person. To properly consider interdependence, for each person in the analysis one needs simultaneous information on his or her access to *all* key goods and services being considered. Because many opportunities are age specific, such as attending school at age 10 and completing sixth grade at age 13, a longitudinal survey or a survey with a considerable amount of retrospective information would be required.

Given the lack of such information among Latin American countries and for simplicity, we opted for reversing the order of aggregation. We first aggregate each dimension (such as the opportunity of access to water) across people, and later we aggregate dimensions. Certainly we could aggregate first a proxy of the five indicators considered in this study, and we plan to do this exercise in the very near future. However, one of the main advantages of the HOI is its flexibility to track progress in a variety of basic goods and services. In country-specific works we can combine information from different sources such as health surveys, living standard measurements surveys, and student assessment test scores, among others. For keeping this flexibility, we would like to have as our base procedure a simple methodology that will allow us to combine information from different sources in building an overall HOI.

If the indicators are continuous, a variety of other alternative aggregation procedures would be available. These alternatives would include weighted versions of the three approaches introduced above as well as completely different function forms. For instance, an expression mimicking a constant elasticity of substitution function could be used.

Notes

1. It should be noted that increasing opportunities sometimes does not require access to goods and services. For instance, to the extent that international migration represents a chance for progress, the right to migrate may be an opportunity in itself. Migration may have private costs, but if they are substantially outweighed by the benefits, it will be the lack of rights that will deter migration and consequent advancement. Many civil rights represent chances to progress and hence opportunities, without necessarily being associated with the access to any key goods or services. We do not dwell here on these types of opportunities.

2. Can changing the distribution of circumstances be a valid policy? In the case of circumstances such as gender, religion, ethnicity, or nationality, society has no interest in changing their distribution to reach universal coverage. But society may, for example, want to eliminate the influence of parental income on a child's education, to reduce the intergenerational transmission of poverty. One strategy to do that is through educational policies. Another could be to implement policies to reduce income inequality. A problem of this strategy is

that equalizing opportunities through reducing inequalities in the distribution of circumstances is often impractical or might take too long.

3. When considering even a small number of circumstances, the number of relevant circumstance groups in a particular society can be very large. For example, consider the case of a society with only six relevant circumstances: gender (male-female), race (white-black), location (urban-rural), parental education (less than primary-primary-secondary-tertiary), and per-capita family income (classified in quintiles). In this particular case, with only six circumstances and a very parsimonious breakdown of each, we will have 160 circumstance groups.

4. According to this line of reasoning, universal access to opportunities is just an instrument to ensure minimum outcomes for all. What should be evaluated is not the universal access in itself, but its consequence on ensuring minimum merit outcomes. Accordingly, whenever available, the best option would be a direct measure of these outcomes (percentage of infants surviving or the percentage of eight-year-olds who are literate). Measures based on outcomes are to a large extent at odds with the notion of opportunity as just a chance to progress. In principle, equality of opportunity should not necessarily lead to equality of outcomes or even to a minimum basic outcome for all. However, some of these *outcomes*, such as a minimum learning threshold, may be considered opportunities because they proxy access to a minimum bundle of goods and services that, according to current technology, can produce a minimum learning standard.

5. Strictly speaking, this implies that we will calculate a measure that consists of the average coverage rate of a basic good or service (for example, access to water). This will be adjusted by the degree by which access to this service (water) is allocated according to a principle of equality of opportunity. So in this second step we are concerned with the equality of opportunity of having access to water.

6. The horizontal axis depicts circumstance groups ordered according to the group-specific probability of access to water.

7. The overall coverage rate C is given by $C = \sum_k w_k C_k$, where w_k denotes the population share of circumstance group k and C_k its specific coverage rate. It can be shown that groups with specific coverage rates below (above) average are over- or underweighted relative to their population share. The HOI can be expressed as $\text{HOI} = (1 + \alpha) \times \sum_{k \in V} w_k C_k$, where $V = \{k: C_k < C\}$ denotes the set of all vulnerable circumstance groups and $a = \sum_{k \in V} w_k$ is the population share of vulnerable groups. The extent to which specific coverage rates are over- or underweighted to obtain the HOI depends only on the share of the population in vulnerable groups (circumstance groups with specific coverage rates below average).

8. See annex A1.5 for a brief discussion of alternatives for the aggregation sequence for building the overall HOI.

9. Notice that the relevant average for population A is not the original average, but that using the population weights from population B (table A1.2.2c).

Bibliography

Abou-Ali, Hala. 2003. "The Effect of Water and Sanitation on Child Mortality in Egypt." Environmental Economics Unit, Department of Economics, Göteborg University, Sweden.

Bajak, F. 2007. "In Peru, a Pint-Size Ticket to Learning." *Washington Post*, December 18, A18.

Barros, Ricardo Paes de, Francisco H. G. Ferreira, José Molinas Vega, and Jaime Saavedra Chanduvi. 2009. *Measuring Inequality of Opportunities in Latin America and the Caribbean*. Washington, DC: Palgrave Macmillan and the World Bank.

Barros, Ricardo Paes de, José Molinas Vega, and Jaime Saavedra Chanduvi. 2008. "Measuring Inequality of Opportunities for Children." World Bank, Washington, DC. www.worldbank.org/lacopportunity.

Bourguignon, François, F. H. G. Ferreira, and M. Menéndez. 2007. "Inequality of Opportunity in Brazil." *Review of Income and Wealth* 53(4): 585–618.

Checchi, D., and V. Peragine. 2005. "Regional Disparities and Inequality of Opportunity: The Case of Italy." IZA Discussion Paper No. 1874, Institute for the Study of Labor, Bonn, Germany.

Fuentes, Ricardo, Tobias Pfütze, and Papa Seck. 2006. "A Logistic Analysis of Diarrhea Incidence and Access to Water and Sanitation." Human Development Report Occasional Paper, United Nations Development Fund, New York.

Galiani, Sebastian, Paul J. Gertler, and Ernesto Schargrodsky. 2005. "Water for Life: The Impact of the Privatization of Water Services on Child Mortality." *Journal of Political Economy* 113: 83–120.

Gustavsson, M. 2007. "Educational Benefits from Solar Technology: Access to Solar Electric Services and Changes in Children's Study Routines, Experiences from Eastern Province Zambia." *Energy Policy* 35(2): 122–29.

Kaufman, S., R. Duke, R. Hansen, J. Rogers, R. Schwartz, and M. Trexler. 2000. "Rural Electrification with Solar Energy as a Climate Protection Strategy." Research Report No. 9, Renewable Energy Policy Project, Washington, DC.

Lefranc, A., N. Pistolesi, and A. Trannoy. 2006. "Inequality of Opportunities vs. Inequality of Outcomes: Are Western Societies All Alike?" Working Paper

No. 54, Society for the Study of Economic Inequality, Palma de Mallorca, Spain.

Roemer, John E. 1998. *Equality of Opportunity.* Cambridge, MA: Harvard University Press.

Rutstein, Shea O. 2000. "Factors Associated with Trends in Infant and Child Mortality in Developing Countries during the 1990s." *Bulletin of the World Health Organization* 78(10): 1256–70.

WHO (World Health Organization). 2002. "The World Health Report 2002: Reducing Risks, Promoting Healthy Life." WHO, Geneva.

World Bank. 2006. *World Development Report 2006: Equity and Development.* Washington, DC: World Bank.

CHAPTER 2

The State of Human Opportunities for Children in the Latin America and the Caribbean Region: 1995–2010

Since the mid-1990s, policy makers in Latin America and the Caribbean (LAC) have increased spending on basic social services, reflecting the increased priority placed on these services in poverty reduction and development strategies. To what extent have these efforts translated into improved opportunities for LAC children to access basic social services, regardless of their circumstances? This chapter reviews the Human Opportunity Index (HOI) for children in the region over the last 15 years and assesses how effective countries have equitably expanded access to the basic education and housing services that a child needs to be able to lead a life of his or her choosing.

The results reveal slow but steady progress in the region as a whole, but they also underscore that progress has not been uniform and that children in some countries face significantly higher obstacles. Since 1995, opportunities for children in the LAC region have expanded by 1 percentage point per year. However, it will take a projected 24 years—an entire generation—to achieve universal provision of basic education and housing services in the region, based on the recent pace of progress and 2010 estimates. If current trends continue, Central American countries will take longer on average—36 years—while Andean countries are poised to achieve universality in 18 years.

Countries in the LAC region show significant variation in children's opportunities to access basic services. In Chile, 95 percent of children have an equal opportunity to access basic services, compared with only 52 percent of the children in Honduras. Chile, Uruguay, Mexico, Costa Rica, República Bolivariana de Venezuela, and Argentina all have HOI scores above 85, whereas four Central American countries (Guatemala, El Salvador, Nicaragua, and Honduras) remain below 60. Overall, countries have been more successful in providing equitably allocated opportunities in the area of education than in housing. Just more than four-fifths of the region's children have equal access to basic education services, with the greatest challenges relating to the quality of those services (ability to finish sixth grade on time) compared with access alone (school enrollment). Less than three-fourths of all children have equal opportunities to access basic housing services, with water and sanitation being the most challenging for countries to provide.

What are the main drivers behind inequality of opportunities for children in the region? The results suggest that, among the seven circumstances considered, parental education, income, and location are the most important in determining inequality of opportunity. Parental education has the largest effect on inequality of opportunity for education, which suggests important constraints for intergenerational mobility. Whether a child lives in a rural or urban area and to a lesser extent per capita family income are the most important circumstances affecting equality of opportunity for housing.

Twenty percent of the improvement in the LAC HOI in the last 15 years reflects changes in the seven circumstances of children that are tracked by the study: That is, one-fifth of the change in the HOI is due to the fact that fewer children are in disadvantaged circumstance groups, for example, because parental education improved, per capita family income increased, or families migrated from rural to urban areas.

By contrast, 80 percent of the improvements in the HOI are explained by changes in the likelihood that children with a given set of circumstance (for instance, children who reside in rural areas and have illiterate parents and four siblings) will be able to access basic services. Of that 80 percent, most of the change reflects improved coverage rates for all children (54 percentage points), but only 27 percentage points arise from a reduction in inequality of opportunity—the relative expansion of access to basic services for children in vulnerable circumstance groups vis-à-vis nonvulnerable groups. Improving the targeting policies of basic services to children in vulnerable circumstance groups could lead to a significant rise in the HOI.

This chapter is organized as follows. The next section characterizes the expansion of the HOI across the 19 LAC countries and discusses data sources and methodology. We then discuss the current state of the HOI in the LAC region, the evolution of the HOI over time, and the drivers of this evolution. The final section outlines the forces behind inequality of opportunity, as an input to policy makers to better target policies in favor of excluded circumstance groups.

Progress in Improving Human Opportunities in LAC—Although Universality Remains a Generation Away

Human opportunity in LAC has expanded markedly over the last 15 years. The HOI for the 18 countries surveyed grew by an average of 1 percent per year between 1995 and 2010, reflecting improvements in the overall coverage rate and equity of access, as well as fewer children in disadvantaged circumstance groups (table 2.1).[1] The HOIs are estimated using data from 37 household surveys for 19 LAC countries over a period of more than a decade (circa 1995 and circa 2008) (table A2.1). Together, the surveys represent more than 200 million children from birth to age 16.

The expansion of coverage rates played a larger role in improving the HOI, but the penalty for unequal access to human opportunities also declined, with its negative impact on the overall HOI decreasing from 7 percent circa 1995 to 5 percent circa 2008. The exceptions were Guatemala, Honduras, and Nicaragua, where the penalty either increased marginally or remained constant as little progress was achieved in improving access among opportunity-vulnerable groups relative to non–opportunity-vulnerable groups.

A Generation to Universalize Basic Services in LAC

Based on the recent rates of progress and assuming linear expansion, the region is projected, on average, to take 24 years starting in 2010 to universalize the basic services contained in the overall HOI (table 2.2), thus providing all children with a level playing field.[2] Central America and the Caribbean will take longer than the regional average—36 and 33 years, respectively—whereas the Southern Cone and Andean nations are projected to take on average 17 and 18 years, respectively. Mexico and Brazil will require 6 and 13 years, respectively, to achieve the goal of universal access to basic services.

Table 2.1 HOI, Coverage Rate, and Penalties, circa 1995 and 2008

Country	HOI (circa 1995)	HOI (circa 2010)	Annual change	Coverage rate (circa 1995)	Coverage rate (circa 2010)	Penalty (circa 1995)	Penalty (circa 2010)
Argentina	87 (1998)	88 (2008)	0.18	90	91	3	2
Bolivia		70 (2007)			77		
Brazil	56 (1995)	76 (2008)	1.56	64	81	8	5
Chile	83 (1996)	92 (2006)	0.86	88	94	5	2
Colombia	68 (1997)	79 (2008)	1.00	77	85	9	6
Costa Rica	77 (1994)	88 (2009)	0.73	82	91	5	2
Dominican Republic	64 (2000)	73 (2008)	1.09	72	79	7	6
Ecuador	60 (1995)	76 (2006)	1.48	68	82	8	6
El Salvador	44 (1998)	53 (2007)	0.99	54	61	10	8
Guatemala	43 (2000)	52 (2006)	1.38	52	60	8	8
Honduras	42 (1999)	48 (2006)	0.83	51	57	9	9
Jamaica	68 (1996)	71 (2002)	0.43	73	75	4	4
Mexico	66 (1996)	87 (2008)	1.70	74	90	8	4
Nicaragua	36 (1998)	47 (2005)	1.57	44	56	9	9
Panama	60 (1997)	64 (2003)	0.70	70	73	10	9
Paraguay	61 (1999)	72 (2008)	1.23	69	78	8	6
Peru	55 (1998)	69 (2008)	1.37	66	77	10	7
Uruguay	89 (2006)	91 (2008)	0.64	92	93	3	2
Venezuela, R. B.	83 (1995)	87 (2005)	0.45	87	90	4	3
LAC average	64	73	1.01	71	78	7	5

Source: Authors' calculations based on household surveys.

Note: Actual survey years in parentheses. For values and standard errors of each indicator that makes up the overall HOI, please refer to tables A2.3b and A2.3c for education indicators and tables A2.4b, A2.4c, A2.4d for housing indicators.

Table 2.2   Estimated 2010 Overall HOI and Simulated Arrival Date by Subregion

Country	Estimated HOI 2010	Rate	Simulated years to arrival	Simulated arrival date
Andean countries	81	1.1	17	2027
Colombia	81			
Ecuador	82			
Peru	72			
Venezuela, R. B.	89			
Brazil	79	1.6	13	2023
Caribbean countries	75	0.8	31	2041
Dominican Republic	75			
Jamaica	75			
Central America	63	1.0	37	2047
Costa Rica	89			
El Salvador	56			
Guatemala	57			
Honduras	52			
Nicaragua	55			
Panama	69			
Mexico	90	1.7	6	2016
Southern Cone	88	0.8	15	2025
Argentina	89			
Chile	95			
Paraguay	75			
Uruguay	92			
LAC average	76	1.0	24	2034

Source: Authors' calculations based on household surveys.

The region will take, on average, almost a generation—22 years—to universalize basic education services, based on the 2010 levels and recent growth rates (table 2.3). Mexico is expected to universalize access to education opportunities within the next decade, and the Andean countries will follow by 2023. Central American countries and Brazil will take longer than the LAC average—27 years—but the Southern Cone countries will require 36 years to reach an education HOI of 100. Looking at the two basic services contained in the education component of the HOI—completing sixth grade on time and attending school for 10 to 14-year-olds—suggests that the greatest challenges are in completing sixth grade on time, especially in Central American countries and in Brazil.

The LAC region will take, on average, approximately 24 years to universalize access to the three basic services included in the housing HOI—access to water, sanitation, and electricity—based on 2010 levels

Table 2.3   Estimated 2010 HOI for Education and Simulated Arrival Date by Subregion

| Country | 2010 estimates of HOI for | | | | Simulated years to arrival | Simulated arrival date |
	Sixth grade on time	School enrollment	Education	Rate		
Andean countries	79	93	86	1.1	13	2023
Colombia	74	94	84			
Ecuador	85	88	87			
Peru	79	96	87			
Venezuela, R. B.	79	96	87			
Brazil	38	99	68	1.2	27	2037
Caribbean countries	77	96	87	0.6	22	2032
Dominican Republic	57	96	77			
Jamaica	97	96	96			
Central America	52	91	71	1.1	27	2037
Costa Rica	67	96	82			
El Salvador	47	92	70			
Guatemala	30	85	57			
Honduras	52	87	70			
Nicaragua	41	91	66			
Panama	74	93	84			
Mexico	90	94	92	1.1	7	2017
Southern Cone	77	95	86	0.4	36	2046
Argentina	82	97	89			
Chile	85	99	92			
Paraguay	59	92	75			
Uruguay	81	94	88			
LAC average	68	94	81	0.9	22	2032

Source: Authors' calculations based on household surveys.

and recent growth rates (table 2.4). Brazil and Mexico are expected to universalize access to housing services within the next decade, and the Southern Cone countries are posed to achieve universal access by 2020 and the Andean countries by 2032. In contrast, it will take the Central American and Caribbean countries almost two generations (45 and 40 years, respectively) to provide full coverage to all children to basic opportunities in housing.

Opportunities for Children to Access Basic Services in the LAC Region

The distribution of human opportunities estimated for 2010 is highly varied across the region. The playing field is almost level for children in

Table 2.4 Estimated 2010 HOI for Housing and Simulated Arrival Date by Subregion

Country	2010 estimated HOIs for				Rate	Simulated years to arrival	Simulated arrival date
	Water	Electricity	Sanitation	Housing			
Andean countries	67	90	70	76	1.1	22	2032
Colombia	54	100	79	78			
Ecuador	84	94	55	78			
Peru	44	68	59	57			
Venezuela, R. B.	88	99	86	91			
Brazil	86	99	84	90	2.0	5	2015
Caribbean countries	45	99	45	63	0.9	40	2050
Dominican Republic	72	98	52	74			
Jamaica	18	100	39	53			
Central America	48	73	43	55	1.0	45	2055
Costa Rica	96	99	94	96			
El Salvador	18	89	19	42			
Guatemala	70	75	27	57			
Honduras	23	56	22	34			
Nicaragua	16	55	59	44			
Panama	63	66	34	54			
Mexico	88	100	76	88	2.3	5	2015
Southern Cone	90	99	77	89	1.1	10	2020
Argentina	98	100	66	88			
Chile	98	100	94	98			
Paraguay	73	97	51	74			
Uruguay	93	99	97	96			
LAC average	66	89	61	72	1.2	24	2034

Source: Authors' calculations based on household surveys.

Chile, where 95 percent of basic housing and education services are available and equitably allocated, whereas in Honduras just over half (52 percent) of the services are available and distributed equitably among children. Chile, Uruguay, Mexico, República Bolivariana de Venezuela, Costa Rica, and Argentina lead the region in moving toward universal access of basic services for their children (figure 2.1). For each of these countries, the estimated 2010 overall HOI is higher than 85, meaning more than 85 percent of the services required for universal coverage are available and allocated equitably. Four countries from Central America are at the bottom of the ranking, with HOIs lower than 60: Honduras, Nicaragua, El Salvador, and Guatemala.

Children in LAC are more likely to have higher levels of equitably allocated services in education than housing: The HOI for education in the region is 81 compared with 72 for housing. Moreover, a wider range is seen in accessing services equitably for housing than for education across countries in LAC.

The education HOI ranges from a high of 96 for Jamaica to a low of 57 for Guatemala, which suggests that children face a nearly level playing field in accessing education in Jamaica, whereas only slightly more than half of education services are available and equitably distributed in Guatemala. Eleven out of the 19 countries analyzed have an education HOI higher than 80. Chile, Jamaica, and Mexico each have an estimated education HOI higher than 90 for 2010.

Comparing the two indicators in the education HOI shows that countries in the region face more challenges in equitably ensuring that children complete sixth grade on time than ensuring that all children aged 10 to 14 attend school regardless of circumstances. Although the average HOI for school enrollment is 94, the average HOI for completing sixth grade on time is only 68.

Similarly, the dispersion of the HOI for completing sixth grade on time is much higher than for school enrollment. Although the HOI for completing sixth grade on time ranges from a high HOI of 97 for Jamaica to a low of 30 for Guatemala, the HOI for school enrollment ranges from 99 for Brazil and Chile to 85 for Guatemala in 2010. The leaders of the HOI for completing sixth grade on time are Chile, Ecuador, Jamaica, and Mexico, each with an HOI at or higher than 85. By contrast, Brazil, El Salvador, Guatemala, and Nicaragua have HOIs lower than 50 for this indicator.

The housing HOI presents higher dispersion than the overall HOI, underscoring the uneven rates of progress in expanding opportunities for

Figure 2.1 Ranking of the Overall HOI, 2010

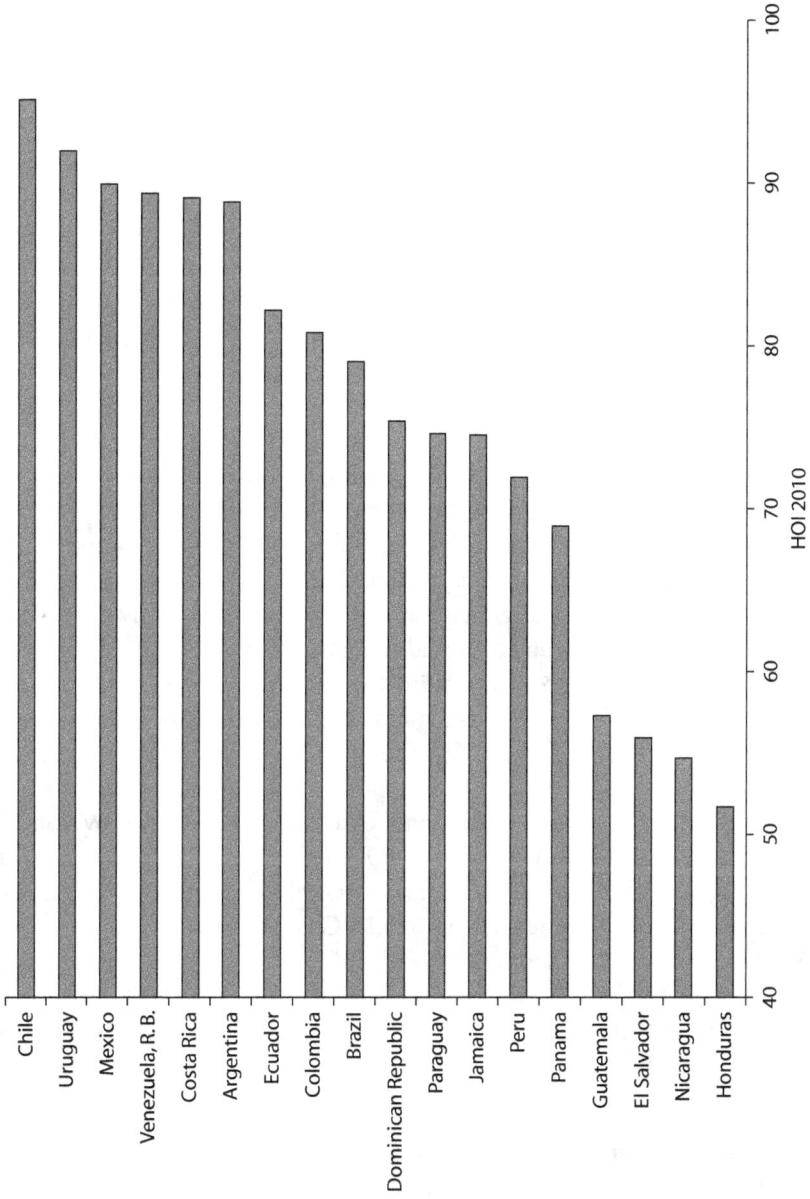

Source: Authors' calculations based on household surveys.

quality housing in LAC. The housing HOI is nearly universal in Chile (98), but it dips to as low as 34 in Honduras, indicating that only one-third of the housing services are available and equitably allocated. Four countries in the region have achieved coverage rates in housing services adjusted for equality of opportunity at or above 90 in 2010: Chile, Costa Rica, Uruguay, and República Bolivariana de Venezuela. Only seven countries out of the 19 considered have a housing HOI higher than 80.

Disaggregating the housing HOI reveals that LAC countries have been more successful in providing children with equitable access to electricity than in delivering equitable opportunities for children to live in homes with clean water and sanitation. Although the average HOI for electricity is 89, the regional averages for water and sanitation opportunities are substantially lower, at 66 and 61, respectively. Thus, at least one-third of the region's children do not have equitable access to water and sanitation opportunities.

Opportunities to access water, sanitation, and electricity in the region are also more widely dispersed compared with educational opportunities. The sanitation HOI ranges from a high of 97 in Uruguay to a low of 19 in El Salvador, and the water HOI ranges from 98 in Argentina and Chile to 16 for Nicaragua. This means that in El Salvador and Nicaragua fewer than one out of five children have an equal opportunity to live in homes with access to both clean water and sanitation. For electricity, Argentina, Chile, Jamaica, and Mexico are estimated to have achieved universal provision by 2010, whereas Nicaragua has an electricity HOI of 55, indicating that just over half of children have equitably distributed access to electricity.

Argentina, Chile, Costa Rica, and Uruguay lead in the provision of opportunities to access water, with HOIs higher than 90. By contrast, El Salvador, Jamaica, and Nicaragua have HOIs lower than 20 for this service. In sanitation, the leaders are Chile, Costa Rica, and Uruguay with HOIs higher than 90, compared with HOIs below 50 for El Salvador, Guatemala, Honduras, Jamaica, and Panama. In electricity, 12 countries out the 19 considered display an HOI higher than 90, and no country has an electricity HOI lower than 55.

Expanding Human Opportunities in Latin America and the Caribbean: 1995–2010

Over the last 15 years, LAC countries have expanded children's opportunities for basic education and housing services. The overall HOI has grown at an average pace of 1 percentage point per year since the mid-1990s (table 2.5). Overall sanitation and completing sixth grade on time indicators saw the largest gains, with annual HOI growth rates of 1.3 points each. School enrollment and electricity, both of which have higher levels of HOIs, had smaller growth rates of 0.5 and 1 point per year, respectively.

Mexico showed the highest rate of improvement in the overall HOI, at 1.7 points per year, compared with a low of 0.3 points per year in Argentina. The five indicators that make up the overall HOI show more variation over time, with expansion rates as high as 4.5 points annually for the sanitation HOI in Nicaragua and 4 points for the water HOI in Ecuador and Mexico. The fastest rate of expansion of the HOI for electricity was 1.9 points annually in El Salvador. In education, the fastest expansion of the HOI for completing sixth grade on time was 2.2 points annually in Peru and 1.3 points annually for the school enrollment HOI in Honduras.

Unpacking Changes in the HOI: Scale, Equity, and Evolving Circumstances

Understanding what is behind the changes in the HOI is important for policy makers interested in leveling the playing field for children and ensuring that they are equipped to pursue a life of their choosing. The sources of expansion of the HOI can be classified into two main groups: (1) changes in circumstance group-specific coverage rates and (2) changes in population shares among the circumstance groups. Because the HOI is completely determined by the specific coverage rates and population shares, as discussed in chapter 1, the HOI can change only when at least one of these elements changes. We refer to changes in the HOI due to changes in the distribution of circumstances as the *composition effect*. Changes in the HOI associated with changes in the group-specific coverage rates are referred to as the *coverage effect*.

Coverage Effects Drove Changes in the HOI

Twenty percent of the improvement in the HOI can be explained by changes in the average circumstances of children in LAC, such as increased residence in urban areas and higher parental education and income levels. The remaining 80 percent of the observed expansion in the HOI reflects gains in group-specific coverage rates for housing and education services (table 2.6). Changes in the likelihood that children with a given set of circumstances (for instance, children who reside in rural areas

Table 2.5 Growth Rates by Indicators, Dimensions, and Overall HOI

Country	Finished sixth grade on time	School enrollment	Education	Water	Electricity	Sanitation	Housing	Overall HOI
Argentina	−0.17	−0.02	−0.10	0.24	—	1.02	0.63	0.26
Brazil	1.53	0.81	1.17	1.61	1.17	3.08	1.95	1.56
Chile	0.81	0.11	0.46	1.08	0.71	1.96	1.25	0.86
Colombia	1.88	0.65	1.27	−0.22	1.22	1.19	0.73	1.00
Costa Rica	0.61	0.75	0.68	0.25	0.51	1.56	0.77	0.73
Dominican Republic	1.87	−0.06	0.91	0.90	1.48	1.44	1.27	1.09
Ecuador	1.35	0.62	0.98	4.06	0.88	0.95	1.97	1.48
El Salvador	1.60	0.92	1.26	0.02	1.87	0.23	0.71	0.99
Guatemala	1.31	1.11	1.21	1.40	1.70	1.54	1.55	1.38
Honduras	1.73	1.30	1.52	0.94	0.68	−0.93	0.23	0.87
Jamaica	0.52	0.10	0.31	−0.63	1.85	0.43	0.55	0.43
Mexico	1.66	0.60	1.13	3.98	0.65	2.16	2.27	1.70
Nicaragua	1.48	1.24	1.36	0.30	0.54	4.52	1.79	1.57
Panama	0.48	0.32	0.40	1.80	0.88	0.35	1.01	0.70
Paraguay	1.21	0.12	0.67	2.76	1.23	1.41	1.80	1.23
Peru	2.24	0.30	1.27	0.45	1.66	2.31	1.47	1.37
Uruguay	1.40	−0.43	0.48	1.96	0.30	0.14	0.80	0.64
Venezuela, R. B.	1.13	0.25	0.69	0.04	0.04	0.55	0.21	0.45
LAC average	1.26	0.50	0.87	1.16	1.02	1.33	1.16	1.02

Source: Authors' calculations based on household surveys.

Note: — = data not available.

Table 2.6 Share of Composition Effect in Total Change of HOIs

	Finished sixth grade on time	School enrollment	Education	Water	Electricity	Sanitation	Housing	Overall HOI
Composition effect (percentage points)	0.3	0.1	**0.2**	0.3	0.0	0.3	**0.2**	0.2
Total change (percentage points)	1.3	0.5	**0.9**	1.2	1.0	1.3	**1.2**	1.0
Share of composition effect (%)	26	27	**26**	23	–2	22	**15**	20
Share of coverage effect (%)	74	73	**74**	77	102	78	**85**	80

Source: Authors' calculations based on household surveys.

and have illiterate parents and four siblings) will be able to access basic services (the coverage effect) dominate the expansion of all the HOIs considered.

The growing access to education opportunities and the increased equality of those opportunities reflects mainly improvements in overall provision as well as the equitable allocation of education services. Circumstances of the average child, due to past improvements in educational opportunities (parental education), overall economic growth (higher parental income), and/or the growing use of income transfer programs, had a much smaller role.[3]

The coverage effects contributed roughly three-fourths of the expansion of the HOI for school enrollment among countries in the LAC region (table 2.7). In eight countries, the coverage effect had a more prominent role; in nine other countries the composition effect was more

Table 2.7   Expansion of Human Opportunity Indices in Education: Contributions of the Composition and Coverage Effects

percentage points

	Finished sixth grade on time			School enrollment (ages 10–14)		
Country	Total change	Composition effect	Coverage effect	Total change	Composition effect	Coverage effect
Argentina	−0.2	0.3	−0.4	0.0	0.1	−0.1
Brazil	1.5	0.4	1.1	0.8	0.3	0.5
Chile	0.8	0.5	0.4	0.1	0.1	0.0
Colombia	1.9	0.4	1.4	0.7	0.2	0.4
Costa Rica	0.6	0.5	0.1	0.7	0.3	0.5
Dominican Republic	1.9	0.4	1.5	−0.1	0.0	−0.1
Ecuador	1.3	−0.8	2.2	0.6	0.5	0.1
El Salvador	1.6	−0.5	2.1	0.9	−0.4	1.3
Guatemala	1.3	0.4	0.9	1.1	0.2	0.9
Honduras	1.7	0.2	1.5	1.3	−0.1	1.4
Jamaica	0.5	0.1	0.4	0.1	0.0	0.1
Mexico	1.7	0.9	0.7	0.6	0.4	0.2
Nicaragua	1.5	0.1	1.4	1.2	−0.1	1.4
Panama	0.5	0.6	−0.1	0.3	0.3	0.1
Paraguay	1.2	0.6	0.6	0.1	0.1	0.0
Peru	2.2	0.6	1.7	0.3	0.2	0.1
Uruguay	1.4	0.5	0.9	−0.4	0.2	−0.7
Venezuela, R. B.	1.1	0.7	0.4	0.3	0.2	0.1
LAC average	1.3	0.3	0.9	0.5	0.1	0.4

Source: Authors' calculations based on household surveys.

prominent. In two countries these two effects contributed equally (Brazil and Guatemala), and in one country these effects were of similar magnitude but in opposite directions (Argentina and the Dominican Republic). In El Salvador, Honduras, and Nicaragua, circumstance groups with lower coverage rates increased their population shares, making the composition effect negative.

The composition effect was less prominent in the housing HOI (table 2.8). The composition effect had a larger contribution than the coverage effect on expanding the water HOI in only 6 out of 18 countries considered. Similarly, the composition effect had a larger contribution than the composition effect in only 5 out of 18 countries in the case of the sanitation HOI, and only 6 out of 18 countries in the case of the electricity HOI. In each of these indicators the coverage effect was more prominent and is discussed further in the following section.

The Equalization and Scale Effects

The coverage effect—the contribution of changes in the coverage rates of different circumstance groups—can be further decomposed into the equalization and scale effects. The scale effect captures the impact of proportional change in coverage rates for all circumstance groups, whereas the equalization effect captures improved coverage rates specifically for circumstance groups with below-average coverage rates vis-à-vis groups with above-average coverage rates. The equalization effect is at the heart of equality of opportunities. A society that wants to level the playing field will focus on expanding opportunities mainly for the vulnerable circumstance groups, and the equalization effect is a clear indicator of progress toward this goal.

Twenty-seven percent of overall HOI change was due to increased equality of opportunity—the equalization effect—in the sample of 18 LAC countries considered during the period covered:[4] that is, improved targeting of basic services to children in vulnerable circumstance groups accounted for about 27 percent of overall improvement. About 22 percent of the change of the HOI for education is due to increased equality of opportunity (21 percent in completing sixth grade on time and 13 percent on school attendance for ages 10–14). About 32 percent of the change of the HOI for housing is due to increased equality of opportunity (23 percent in water, 26 percent in sanitation, and 33 percent in electricity). Equality of opportunity could accelerate more quickly if services were better targeted to underserved circumstance groups in the region.

Table 2.8 Expansion of the Human Opportunity Indices in Housing: Contributions of the Composition and Coverage Effects

percentage points

Country	Water			Sanitation			Electricity		
	Total change	Composition effect	Coverage effect	Total change	Composition effect	Coverage effect	Total change	Composition effect	Coverage effect
Argentina	0.2	0.2	0.0	1.0	1.2	-0.2	—	—	—
Brazil	1.6	0.9	0.7	3.1	1.2	1.9	1.2	0.6	0.6
Chile	1.1	0.7	0.4	2.0	1.0	1.0	0.7	0.4	0.3
Colombia	-0.2	0.3	-0.6	1.2	0.4	0.8	1.2	0.8	0.4
Costa Rica	0.2	0.0	0.2	1.6	0.6	1.0	0.5	0.2	0.3
Dominican Republic	0.9	0.3	0.6	1.4	0.2	1.2	1.5	0.4	1.1
Ecuador	4.1	-2.0	6.0	1.0	-3.1	4.1	0.9	-4.0	4.9
El Salvador	0.0	-1.0	1.0	0.2	-1.0	1.2	1.9	-1.3	3.1
Guatemala	1.4	0.5	0.9	1.5	0.7	0.9	1.7	0.6	1.1
Honduras	0.9	0.0	0.9	-0.9	-0.2	-0.7	0.7	0.0	0.7
Jamaica	-0.6	-0.1	-0.5	0.4	0.0	0.5	1.9	-0.2	2.1
Mexico	4.0	1.4	2.6	2.2	1.8	0.4	0.7	0.4	0.3
Nicaragua	0.3	-0.2	0.5	4.5	-0.1	4.6	0.5	-0.4	1.0
Panama	1.8	0.4	1.4	0.3	0.7	-0.3	0.9	0.9	-0.1
Paraguay	2.8	0.5	2.3	1.4	0.4	1.0	1.2	0.3	0.9
Peru	0.4	0.4	0.1	2.3	0.4	1.9	1.7	0.5	1.2
Uruguay	2.0	1.9	0.1	0.1	0.6	-0.4	0.3	0.3	0.0
Venezuela, R. B.	0.0	0.6	-0.6	0.5	0.6	0.0	0.0	0.1	0.0
LAC average	1.2	0.3	0.9	1.3	0.3	1.0	1.0	0.0	1.0

Source: Authors' calculations based on household surveys.

Note: — = data not available.

The expansion of the education HOI due to the coverage effect is on the whole dominated by the scale effect (table 2.9); that is, improved coverage rates came mainly by increasing education service provision for the entire population, not necessarily more to those who were previously underserved. However, there are 5 cases out of 36 (18 countries for each of the two basic opportunities considered) where the equalization effect is the same size as the scale effect, and 2 cases where the equalization effect is a bit bigger than the scale effect (Guatemala and Panama for completion of sixth grade on time).

The scale effect also is generally dominant for changes of the housing HOI driven by the coverage effect (table 2.10). This indicates that, in housing as well, progress has mainly been achieved through greater overall coverage rates, rather than improved targeting to reach children in

Table 2.9 Coverage Effect in Education Human Opportunity Indices: Contributions of the Equalization and Scale Effects

percentage points

Country	Finished sixth grade on time			School attendance (ages 10–14)		
	Total coverage effect	Equalization effect	Scale effect	Total coverage effect	Equalization effect	Scale effect
Argentina	−0.4	−0.1	−0.4	−0.1	0.0	−0.1
Brazil	1.1	0.4	0.7	0.5	0.2	0.4
Chile	0.4	0.1	0.2	0.0	0.0	0.0
Colombia	1.4	0.6	0.8	0.4	0.1	0.3
Costa Rica	0.1	0.0	0.0	0.5	0.1	0.4
Dominican Republic	1.5	0.4	1.0	−0.1	0.0	−0.1
Ecuador	2.2	0.6	1.6	0.1	0.0	0.0
El Salvador	2.1	0.6	1.5	1.3	0.3	1.0
Guatemala	0.9	0.5	0.4	0.9	0.1	0.7
Honduras	1.5	0.3	1.2	1.4	0.3	1.1
Jamaica	0.4	0.1	0.4	0.1	0.0	0.1
Mexico	0.7	0.2	0.5	0.2	0.1	0.1
Nicaragua	1.4	0.3	1.1	1.4	0.4	1.0
Panama	−0.1	0.0	−0.2	0.1	0.0	0.1
Paraguay	0.6	0.2	0.5	0.0	0.0	0.0
Peru	1.7	0.5	1.2	0.1	0.1	0.1
Uruguay	0.9	0.2	0.7	−0.7	−0.2	−0.5
Venezuela, R. B.	0.4	0.1	0.3	0.1	0.0	0.1
LAC average	0.9	0.3	0.6	0.3	0.1	0.3

Source: Authors' calculations based on household surveys.
Note: For values in percent terms, please refer to annex table A2.10.

Table 2.10 Coverage Effect in Housing Human Opportunity Indices: Contributions of the Equalization and Scale Effects

percentage points

Country	Water			Sanitation					Electricity		
	Total coverage effect	Equalization effect	Scale effect	Total coverage effect	Equalization effect	Scale effect	Total coverage effect	Equalization effect	Scale effect		
Argentina	0.0	0.0	0.0	−0.2	0.0	−0.2	—	—	—		
Brazil	0.7	0.3	0.4	1.9	0.5	1.4	0.6	0.2	0.3		
Chile	0.4	0.2	0.2	1.0	0.4	0.6	0.3	0.1	0.2		
Colombia	−0.6	0.0	−0.5	0.8	0.4	0.4	0.4	0.2	0.2		
Costa Rica	0.2	0.0	0.2	1.0	0.3	0.6	0.3	0.1	0.2		
Dominican Republic	0.6	0.2	0.4	1.2	0.4	0.9	1.1	0.4	0.7		
Ecuador	6.0	2.6	3.5	4.1	1.4	2.7	4.9	2.1	2.8		
El Salvador	1.0	0.1	0.9	1.2	0.3	0.9	3.1	1.2	1.9		
Guatemala	0.9	0.3	0.6	0.9	0.3	0.5	1.1	0.4	0.6		
Honduras	0.9	0.4	0.6	−0.7	−0.4	−0.3	0.7	0.3	0.4		
Jamaica	−0.5	−0.2	−0.3	0.5	0.1	0.4	2.1	0.3	1.7		
Mexico	2.6	1.0	1.6	0.4	0.0	0.4	0.3	0.1	0.2		
Nicaragua	0.5	0.1	0.4	4.6	2.4	2.2	1.0	0.3	0.7		
Panama	1.4	0.5	0.9	−0.3	0.0	−0.3	−0.1	0.0	−0.1		
Paraguay	2.3	0.9	1.3	1.0	0.3	0.7	0.9	0.3	0.6		
Peru	0.1	0.1	0.0	1.9	0.9	1.0	1.2	0.5	0.7		
Uruguay	0.1	−0.1	0.2	−0.4	−0.1	−0.3	0.0	0.0	0.0		
Venezuela, R. B.	−0.6	−0.1	−0.5	0.0	0.0	0.0	0.0	0.0	0.0		
LAC average	0.9	0.3	0.6	1.0	0.4	0.6	1.0	0.4	0.7		

Source: Authors' calculations based on household surveys.

Note: For values in percent terms, please refer to appendix table A2.11. — = data not available.

underserved circumstance groups. However, in three out of 53 cases (18 countries for access to water and sanitation, and 17 countries for access to electricity), the equalization effect dominates: Peru, in the case of water, and Honduras and Nicaragua, in the case of sanitation. In the case of access to sanitation in Honduras, the overall coverage effect has been contractive: that is, changes in the coverage specific rates, especially reduced coverage among the vulnerable groups, have contributed to reducing the HOI for sanitation in Honduras.

In summary, only rarely has the equalization effect played a more prominent role within the coverage effect. The default situation seems to be a dominance of the scale effect. In only four cases (out of 89 considered) does the equalization effect dominate and have a positive effect. This indicates that Latin American countries could make far more effective use of their resources to provide basic opportunities to their children by improving the targeting of social service provision to those most in need.

The Inequality of Opportunity Profile

To level the playing field for all children, policy makers need to know the equality-of-opportunity profile for a given society to design effective public policies for accelerating the equitable expansion of human opportunities. This section analyzes the main circumstances affecting equality of opportunity for access to a basic service and the relative effect on this opportunity of a specific circumstance—such as gender, where a child lives, or their parent's income—compared with other circumstances.

The equality of opportunity measure D—the methodology for which is explained in chapter 1—is a synthetic measure that aggregates the differences in coverage among all groups arising from a defined set of circumstances.[5] In addition, it is also possible to measure the equality of opportunity associated with only one specific circumstance. For policy design, it may be important to analyze how each circumstance contributes to overall inequality of opportunity. Moreover, a constant level of overall equality of opportunity over time may hide important changes. For example, equality of opportunity in education resulting from urban or rural location may be increasing, while inequality of opportunity in education resulting from differences in a parent's education may be declining.

To compute the synthetic D-index, all circumstances are considered simultaneously. An equality-of-opportunity profile can also be defined by computing a specific D-index for each circumstance (gender, parent's education, and so forth) and then comparing them to identify which specific circumstances elicit larger inequality in a given basic good or service. Complementary ways are used to report an equality-of-opportunity profile for the LAC region: (1) a profile based on the average D-indices in the region and (2) a profile based on the number of countries where one specific circumstance is more important in characterizing existing equality of opportunity.

A specific D-index can be computed for each of the seven circumstances for each of the basic goods and services considered, averaged across the LAC region (table 2.11; country results are reported in tables A2.5–A2.9). These numbers represent the proportion of the available basic good or service that would have to be redistributed among children for equality of opportunity to prevail, if only one circumstance was considered. For example, for access to water, the average D-indices calculated for each circumstance range from 0.4 percent for gender of the child to 11 percent for area of residence. Hence, if the only circumstance considered is area of residence, 11 percent of available water connections need to be reallocated to eliminate the differences in access to water across different groups. When considering a child's gender, only 0.4 percent of available water connections need to be reallocated in LAC to eliminate the differences in access to water.

The inequality-of-opportunity profile for education shows that in LAC, parental education and income continue to influence whether a child has fair access to education opportunities. In short, parental characteristics affect the ability of a child to improve his or her situation over time and achieve intergenerational mobility. For completing sixth grade on time, the most important circumstance in LAC countries is parental

Table 2.11   *D*-Index by Circumstance and Opportunity, circa 2010

Circumstance	Finished sixth grade on time	School attendance	Water	Sanitation	Electricity
Parent's education	6.5	1.2	4.7	7.5	1.4
Gender	3.1	0.3	0.4	0.3	0.1
Gender of household head	1.3	0.3	1.6	2.2	0.5
Per capita income	2.7	0.4	6.2	8.3	1.8
Urban or rural	2.3	0.4	10.9	13.8	3.9
Presence of parents	1.2	0.4	0.9	1.3	0.1
Number of siblings	3.0	0.2	1.3	1.8	0.4

Source: Authors' calculations based on household surveys.

education, and to a lesser extent the gender of the child and number of siblings. A complementary profile, based on the number of countries where one specific D-index dominates, confirms these findings. Parental education dominates the rankings in 17 out of 18 countries, and the number of siblings dominates the rankings in one country (table A2.5).

For school enrollment for children aged 10–14, the inequality-of-opportunity profile is also driven mainly by parental education. The profile based on number of countries shows that parental education dominates the rankings in 15 countries. The presence of two parents in a child's household tops the rankings in two countries, and per capita family income dominates in one country (table A2.6).

For access to water, sanitation, and electricity, the inequality-of-opportunity profile is driven mainly by where a child lives (rural versus urban residence) and to lesser extent by per capita family income. In the profile based on number of countries, the location circumstance dominates the rankings in 13 countries (out of 18) in the case of water, 12 countries in sanitation, and 16 countries (out of 17, Argentina excluded) in the case of electricity (tables A2.7–A2.9).

Annex

Table A2.1 Surveys Used to Calculate the HOI

Country	Circa 1995	Circa 2010	Coverage	Survey
Argentina	1998	2008	Urban	Encuesta Permanente de Hogares
Bolivia	—	2007	National	Encuesta Continua de Hogares
Brazil	1995	2008	National	Pesquisa Nacional por Amostra de Domicílios
Chile	1996	2006	National	Encuesta de Caracterización Socioeconómica Nacional
Colombia	1997	2008	National	Encuesta de Calidad de Vida
Costa Rica	1994	2009	National	Encuesta de Hogares de Propósitos Múltiples
Dominican Republic	2000	2008	National	Encuesta Nacional de Fuerza de Trabajo
Ecuador	1995	2006	National	Encuesta de Condiciones de Vida
El Salvador	1998	2007	National	Encuesta de Hogares de Propósitos Múltiples
Guatemala	2000	2006	National	Encuesta Nacional sobre Condiciones de Vida
Honduras	1999	2006	National	Encuesta Permanente de Hogares de Propósitos Múltiples
Jamaica	1996	2002	National	Jamaica Survey of Living Conditions
Mexico	1996	2008	National	Encuesta Nacional de Ingresos y Gastos de los Hogares
Nicaragua	1998	2005	National	Encuesta Nacional de Hogares sobre Medición de Nivel de Vida
Panama	1997	2003	National	Encuesta de Niveles de Vida
Paraguay	1999	2008	National	Encuesta Permanente de Hogares
Peru	1998	2008	National	Encuesta Nacional de Hogares
Uruguay	2006	2008	National	Encuesta Nacional de Hogares Ampliada
Venezuela, R. B.	1995	2005	National	Encuesta de Hogares por Muestreo

Source: World Bank and Universidad de La Plata (CEDLAS) Socioeconomic Database for Latin America and the Caribbean.

Note: — = data not available.

Table A2.2 Overall HOI and Decomposition (1995 and 2010)

Country	Opportunity index (%)				Annual rate of change (percentage points)	Decomposition (percentage points)				Decomposition (%)				Extrapolation (%)	
							Coverage effect				Coverage effect				
	Circa 1995	If the population of 2010 lived in 1995	Considering the inequality of 2010 and the average probability of 1995	Circa 2010		Composition effect	Total	Equalization effect	Scale effect	Composition effect	Total	Equalization effect	Scale effect	1995	2010
Argentina	86.7	86.9	86.8	88.5	0.2	0.02	0.16	−0.01	0.17	10	90	−5	95	86.2	88.8
Brazil	55.6	63.7	67.8	75.9	1.6	0.62	0.94	0.31	0.63	40	60	20	40	55.6	79.0
Chile	83.1	87.9	89.4	91.7	0.9	0.48	0.37	0.15	0.23	56	44	17	27	82.2	95.1
Colombia	68.3	72.8	75.8	79.3	1.0	0.42	0.58	0.27	0.31	42	58	27	31	66.3	81.2
Costa Rica	77.4	82.5	84.2	88.3	0.7	0.34	0.39	0.11	0.28	47	53	15	38	78.1	89.0
Dominican Republic	64.5	66.5	68.6	73.2	1.1	0.25	0.84	0.27	0.57	23	77	25	53	59.0	75.4
Ecuador	60.0	42.5	55.3	76.2	1.5	−1.59	3.07	1.17	1.90	−108	208	79	129	60.0	82.1
El Salvador	44.1	37.2	41.6	52.9	1.0	−0.76	1.75	0.49	1.26	−78	178	50	128	41.1	55.9
Guatemala	43.5	46.3	48.3	51.8	1.4	0.47	0.91	0.32	0.59	34	66	23	42	36.6	57.3
Honduras	42.1	42.0	43.5	48.2	0.9	−0.02	0.89	0.21	0.68	−2	102	24	78	38.6	51.7
Jamaica	68.5	68.2	68.6	71.1	0.4	−0.04	0.47	0.06	0.41	−10	110	14	95	68.1	74.5
Mexico	66.2	77.3	80.4	86.5	1.7	0.93	0.77	0.26	0.51	55	45	15	30	64.5	89.9
Nicaragua	35.8	35.0	39.4	46.8	1.6	−0.11	1.68	0.62	1.06	−7	107	39	68	31.1	54.7
Panama	59.8	63.1	63.7	64.0	0.7	0.55	0.15	0.10	0.06	78	22	14	8	58.4	68.9
Paraguay	61.0	64.4	67.1	72.1	1.2	0.38	0.85	0.29	0.56	31	69	24	46	56.1	74.6
Peru	55.5	59.3	63.2	69.2	1.4	0.38	0.99	0.40	0.59	28	72	29	43	51.3	71.9
Uruguay	89.4	90.7	90.6	90.6	0.6	0.65	−0.01	−0.03	0.02	101	−1	−5	4	82.3	91.9
Venezuela, R. B.	82.5	86.8	86.9	87.1	0.5	0.43	0.02	0.01	0.01	95	5	2	3	82.5	89.3
LAC average	63.5	65.2	67.8	73.0	1.0	0.2	0.8	0.3	0.5	19	81	27	54	61.0	76.2

Source: Authors' calculations based on household surveys.

Table A2.3a HOI in Education and Decomposition (1995 and 2010)

Country	Opportunity index (%)				Annual rate of change (percentage points)	Decomposition (percentage points)				Decomposition (%)				Extrapolation (%)	
	Circa 1995	If the population of 2010 lived in 1995	Considering the inequality of 2010 and the average probability of 1995	Circa 2010		Composition effect	Total	Coverage effect Equalization effect	Scale effect	Composition effect	Total	Coverage effect Equalization effect	Scale effect	1995	2010
Argentina	90.6	92.3	92.0	89.7	−0.1	0.16	−0.26	−0.03	−0.23	−171	271	27	244	90.9	89.5
Brazil	50.9	55.4	59.1	66.1	1.2	0.35	0.82	0.28	0.54	30	70	24	46	50.9	68.4
Chile	85.6	88.3	88.9	90.2	0.5	0.27	0.19	0.06	0.13	59	41	14	28	85.1	92.1
Colombia	67.5	71.1	75.0	81.5	1.3	0.33	0.95	0.36	0.59	26	74	28	46	65.0	84.0
Costa Rica	70.8	76.8	77.8	81.0	0.7	0.40	0.28	0.07	0.21	59	41	10	31	71.5	81.6
Dominican Republic	67.7	69.3	71.1	74.9	0.9	0.21	0.70	0.22	0.48	23	77	24	53	63.1	76.7
Ecuador	71.8	70.1	73.7	82.7	1.0	−0.16	1.14	0.33	0.81	−16	116	34	82	71.8	86.6
El Salvador	54.6	50.4	54.5	65.9	1.3	−0.46	1.72	0.45	1.27	−37	137	36	101	50.8	69.7
Guatemala	45.2	47.2	49.0	52.4	1.2	0.34	0.87	0.30	0.57	28	72	25	47	39.1	57.3
Honduras	52.9	53.2	55.6	63.5	1.5	0.04	1.47	0.34	1.13	3	97	22	75	46.9	69.6
Jamaica	92.1	92.4	92.6	94.0	0.3	0.04	0.27	0.04	0.22	14	86	14	72	91.8	96.5
Mexico	76.0	84.0	85.8	89.6	1.1	0.67	0.46	0.14	0.32	59	41	13	28	74.9	91.8
Nicaragua	49.5	49.5	51.8	59.0	1.4	0.00	1.36	0.32	1.04	0	100	24	77	45.5	65.8
Panama	78.3	81.0	81.1	80.7	0.4	0.44	−0.04	0.02	−0.06	110	−10	4	−14	77.6	83.5
Paraguay	68.1	71.3	72.1	74.1	0.7	0.35	0.32	0.09	0.23	52	48	14	34	65.5	75.5
Peru	71.9	75.4	78.1	84.6	1.3	0.35	0.92	0.28	0.64	28	72	22	50	68.1	87.1
Uruguay	85.6	86.4	86.4	86.6	0.5	0.39	0.10	0.01	0.08	80	20	3	17	80.3	87.6
Venezuela, R. B.	77.1	81.4	82.1	84.0	0.7	0.43	0.26	0.07	0.19	62	38	10	28	77.1	87.5
LAC average	69.8	72.0	73.7	77.8	0.9	0.2	0.6	0.2	0.5	26	74	21	52	67.6	80.6

Source: Authors' calculations based on household surveys.

Table A2.3b HOI for School Enrollment and Decomposition (1995 and 2010)

Country	Opportunity index (%)							Decomposition (percentage points)				Decomposition (%)				Extrapolation (%)	
	Circa 1995		If the population of 2010 lived in 1995	Considering the inequality of 2010 and the average probability of 1995	Circa 2010		Annual rate of change (percentage points)	Composition effect	Coverage effect			Composition effect	Coverage effect				
	Value	Standard error			Value	Standard error			Total	Equalization effect	Scale effect		Total	Equalization effect	Scale effect	1995	2010
Argentina	97.0	0.3	97.6	97.7	96.8	0.4	0.0	0.06	-0.08	0.00	-0.08	-248	348	-6	354	97.1	96.8
Brazil	86.8	0.2	90.2	92.5	97.3	0.1	0.8	0.26	0.54	0.17	0.37	33	67	21	46	86.8	98.9
Chile	97.3	0.2	98.1	98.2	98.4	0.2	0.1	0.08	0.03	0.01	0.02	72	28	8	20	97.2	98.9
Colombia	86.0	0.6	88.4	89.7	93.0	0.4	0.7	0.22	0.43	0.12	0.32	34	66	18	49	84.7	94.3
Costa Rica	84.3	0.7	88.0	89.8	95.5	0.3	0.7	0.25	0.50	0.12	0.38	34	66	16	51	85.0	96.3
Dominican Republic	96.9	0.4	96.9	97.0	96.5	0.4	-0.1	-0.01	-0.05	0.02	-0.07	9	91	-32	123	97.2	96.3
Ecuador	79.0	1.0	84.8	85.3	85.9	0.6	0.6	0.53	0.09	0.05	0.05	85	15	7	8	79.0	88.4
El Salvador	81.1	0.6	77.6	80.2	89.4	0.5	0.9	-0.39	1.31	0.29	1.02	-42	142	32	110	78.3	92.1
Guatemala	73.8	0.9	75.2	76.1	80.4	0.6	1.1	0.24	0.87	0.15	0.73	21	79	13	65	68.2	84.9
Honduras	72.8	0.8	72.1	74.5	82.0	0.4	1.3	-0.11	1.41	0.34	1.07	-8	108	26	82	67.6	87.2
Jamaica	94.4	1.1	94.2	94.4	95.0	0.6	0.1	-0.03	0.13	0.03	0.10	-26	126	30	96	94.3	95.8
Mexico	85.3	0.6	90.3	91.0	92.5	0.4	0.6	0.41	0.18	0.06	0.12	69	31	10	20	84.7	93.7
Nicaragua	75.9	1.0	75.0	77.7	84.6	0.7	1.2	-0.13	1.37	0.39	0.98	-11	111	31	79	72.2	90.7
Panama	88.9	0.7	90.5	90.4	90.8	0.7	0.3	0.26	0.05	-0.01	0.06	83	17	-3	20	88.3	93.0
Paraguay	91.0	0.8	92.0	92.1	92.0	0.7	0.1	0.12	0.00	0.01	-0.01	102	-2	8	-10	90.5	92.3
Peru	92.1	0.5	93.6	94.2	95.0	0.3	0.3	0.15	0.14	0.06	0.09	51	49	19	30	91.2	95.6
Uruguay	95.6	0.2	96.1	95.8	94.8	0.3	-0.4	0.24	-0.68	-0.15	-0.53	-56	156	35	121	100.4	93.9
Venezuela, R. B.	92.1	0.4	93.8	94.0	94.6	0.2	0.3	0.18	0.08	0.02	0.06	70	30	6	24	92.1	95.9
LAC average	87.2		88.6	89.5	91.9		0.5	0.1	0.4	0.1	0.3	27	73	19	54	86.4	93.6

Source: Authors' calculations based on household surveys.

Table A2.3c HOI for Completing Sixth Grade on Time and Decomposition (1995 and 2010)

| | Opportunity index (%) | | | | | | | Decomposition (percentage points) | | | | Decomposition (%) | | | | Extrapolation (%) | |
| | Circa 1995 | | If the population of 2010 lived in 1995 | Considering the inequality of 2010 and the average probability of 1995 | Circa 2010 | | Annual rate of change (percentage points) | | Coverage effect | | | | Coverage effect | | | | |
Country	Value	Standard error	1995		Value	Standard error		Composition effect	Total	Equalization effect	Scale effect	Composition effect	Total	Equalization effect	Scale effect	1995	2010
Argentina	84.3	0.9	87.0	86.4	82.6	1.1	-0.2	0.27	-0.44	-0.05	-0.38	-160	260	32	228	84.8	82.2
Brazil	15.0	0.2	20.6	25.7	34.9	0.3	1.5	0.43	1.10	0.39	0.71	28	72	25	47	15.0	38.0
Chile	73.9	1.0	78.5	79.7	82.0	0.9	0.8	0.46	0.35	0.12	0.24	57	43	14	29	73.1	85.3
Colombia	49.0	0.9	53.7	60.3	70.0	0.9	1.9	0.43	1.44	0.60	0.84	23	77	32	45	45.2	73.8
Costa Rica	57.3	1.0	65.5	65.7	66.4	1.1	0.6	0.55	0.06	0.01	0.04	90	10	2	7	57.9	67.0
Dominican Republic	38.4	1.1	41.8	45.1	53.4	1.1	1.9	0.42	1.46	0.42	1.04	22	78	22	55	29.1	57.2
Ecuador	64.6	1.2	55.4	62.2	79.5	0.8	1.3	-0.84	2.19	0.62	1.57	-63	163	46	117	64.6	84.9
El Salvador	28.1	0.7	23.2	28.8	42.5	0.8	1.6	-0.54	2.14	0.61	1.53	-34	134	38	95	23.3	47.3
Guatemala	16.6	0.7	19.3	22.0	24.4	0.7	1.3	0.45	0.86	0.45	0.41	34	66	35	31	10.0	29.7
Honduras	33.0	0.9	34.4	36.8	45.1	0.5	1.7	0.20	1.53	0.33	1.20	12	88	19	69	26.1	52.0
Jamaica	89.9	2.2	90.5	90.9	93.0	1.0	0.5	0.11	0.41	0.06	0.35	21	79	11	67	89.3	97.2
Mexico	66.8	0.8	77.8	80.5	86.7	0.6	1.7	0.92	0.74	0.23	0.51	56	44	14	31	65.1	90.0
Nicaragua	23.2	1.0	24.1	25.8	33.5	0.8	1.5	0.13	1.35	0.25	1.10	8	92	17	74	18.7	40.9
Panama	67.8	1.1	71.4	71.7	70.6	1.2	0.5	0.61	-0.13	0.04	-0.18	128	-28	9	-37	66.8	74.0
Paraguay	45.3	1.4	50.5	52.1	56.3	1.3	1.2	0.58	0.64	0.17	0.46	47	53	14	38	40.5	58.7
Peru	51.7	1.0	57.2	62.1	74.1	0.6	2.2	0.55	1.69	0.50	1.19	25	75	22	53	44.9	78.6
Uruguay	75.6	0.5	76.7	77.0	78.4	0.6	1.4	0.53	0.87	0.18	0.69	38	62	13	50	60.2	81.2
Venezuela, R. B.	62.2	0.8	69.0	70.2	73.4	0.5	1.1	0.68	0.45	0.13	0.32	60	40	11	28	62.2	79.1
LAC average	52.4		55.4	57.9	63.7		1.3	0.3	0.9	0.3	0.6	26	74	22	51	48.7	67.6

Source: Authors' calculations based on household surveys.

Table A2.4a HOI for Housing Conditions and Decomposition (1995 and 2010)

Country	Opportunity index (%)				Annual rate of change (percentage points)	Decomposition (percentage points)				Decomposition (%)				Extrapolation (%)	
	If the population of 2010 lived in 1995		Considering the inequality of 2010 and the average probability of 1995				Coverage effect				Coverage effect				
	Circa 1995	1995		Circa 2010		Composition effect	Total	Equalization effect	Scale effect	Composition effect	Total	Equalization effect	Scale effect	1995	2010
Argentina	82.8	81.5	81.6	87.3	0.4	-0.13	0.58	0.01	0.57	-29	129	2	127	81.4	88.1
Brazil	60.3	71.9	76.5	85.7	2.0	0.90	1.06	0.35	0.71	46	54	18	36	60.3	89.6
Chile	80.6	87.5	89.8	93.1	1.3	0.69	0.56	0.23	0.33	55	45	18	26	79.3	98.1
Colombia	69.0	74.6	76.6	77.0	0.7	0.51	0.22	0.18	0.04	70	30	25	5	67.5	78.5
Costa Rica	84.1	88.3	90.5	95.7	0.8	0.28	0.49	0.15	0.34	36	64	19	44	84.8	96.5
Dominican Republic	61.2	63.6	66.1	71.4	1.3	0.29	0.98	0.32	0.66	23	77	25	52	54.9	74.0
Ecuador	48.2	14.9	36.9	69.8	2.0	-3.03	4.99	2.00	2.99	-154	254	102	152	48.2	77.7
El Salvador	33.6	24.0	28.7	40.0	0.7	-1.07	1.77	0.52	1.25	-151	251	74	177	31.5	42.1
Guatemala	41.8	45.4	47.5	51.1	1.5	0.60	0.95	0.35	0.60	39	61	22	39	34.1	57.3
Honduras	31.2	30.7	31.3	32.8	0.2	-0.08	0.30	0.09	0.22	-33	133	38	96	30.3	33.7
Jamaica	44.9	44.1	44.6	48.1	0.5	-0.13	0.68	0.08	0.60	-23	123	15	108	44.3	52.5
Mexico	56.3	70.5	75.0	83.5	2.3	1.18	1.08	0.37	0.71	52	48	16	31	54.1	88.0
Nicaragua	22.1	20.5	27.0	34.6	1.8	-0.22	2.01	0.92	1.09	-12	112	52	61	16.7	43.5
Panama	41.2	45.2	46.2	47.3	1.0	0.66	0.35	0.17	0.17	66	34	17	17	39.2	54.3
Paraguay	53.9	57.6	62.0	70.1	1.8	0.41	1.39	0.49	0.90	23	77	27	50	46.7	73.7
Peru	39.1	43.2	48.3	53.8	1.5	0.42	1.06	0.51	0.55	28	72	35	37	34.6	56.7
Uruguay	93.1	94.9	94.8	94.7	0.8	0.91	-0.12	-0.08	-0.04	115	-15	-10	-4	84.3	96.3
Venezuela, R. B.	88.0	92.3	91.7	90.1	0.2	0.43	-0.22	-0.06	-0.16	203	-103	-26	-77	88.0	91.2
LAC average	57.3	58.4	61.9	68.1	1.2	0.1	1.0	0.4	0.6	13.0	87.0	32.0	56.0	54.5	71.8

Source: Authors' calculations based on household surveys.

Table A2.4b HOI for Water and Decomposition (1995 and 2010)

| Country | Opportunity index (%) | | | | | | Annual rate of change (percentage points) | Decomposition (percentage points) | | | | | Decomposition (%) | | | | | Extrapolation (%) | |
| | Circa 1995 | | If the population of 2010 lived in 1995 | Considering the inequality of 2010 and the average probability of 1995 | Circa 2010 | | | Composition effect | Coverage effect | | | Composition effect | | Coverage effect | | | | |
	Value	Standard error			Value	Standard error			Total	Equalization effect	Scale effect		Total	Equalization effect	Scale effect	1995	2010
Argentina	95.0	0.2	96.9	97.0	97.3	0.2	0.2	0.19	0.05	0.01	0.03	80	20	6	14	94.3	97.8
Brazil	61.6	0.1	73.4	76.8	82.5	0.1	1.6	0.91	0.70	0.27	0.44	56	44	16	27	61.6	85.8
Chile	83.1	0.2	89.8	91.7	93.9	0.1	1.1	0.67	0.41	0.18	0.23	62	38	17	21	82.1	98.3
Colombia	57.0	0.4	60.7	60.2	54.0	0.4	−0.2	0.34	−0.56	−0.05	−0.51	−155	255	23	232	57.4	53.6
Costa Rica	91.7	0.3	92.3	92.4	95.4	0.2	0.2	0.04	0.21	0.01	0.20	16	84	4	80	91.9	95.7
Dominican Republic	62.9	0.6	65.5	66.9	70.1	0.5	0.9	0.32	0.57	0.18	0.40	36	64	20	44	58.4	71.9
Ecuador	22.9	0.4	1.1	29.2	67.6	0.4	4.1	−1.98	6.04	2.55	3.49	−49	149	63	86	22.9	83.9
El Salvador	18.1	0.2	9.3	10.1	18.3	0.2	0.0	−0.97	0.99	0.08	0.91	−4,190	4,290	359	3,931	18.0	18.3
Guatemala	55.5	0.5	58.4	60.1	63.9	0.4	1.4	0.48	0.92	0.27	0.64	35	65	20	46	48.5	69.5
Honduras	13.1	0.3	13.2	15.8	19.7	0.2	0.9	0.01	0.92	0.37	0.55	2	98	39	59	9.4	23.4
Jamaica	27.2	1.0	26.4	25.4	23.4	0.6	−0.6	−0.14	−0.49	−0.16	−0.33	22	78	26	53	27.8	18.3
Mexico	32.5	0.3	49.3	61.1	80.3	0.3	4.0	1.40	2.58	0.98	1.59	35	65	25	40	28.5	88.2
Nicaragua	12.7	0.5	11.5	12.1	14.8	0.3	0.3	−0.16	0.46	0.08	0.38	−55	155	28	126	11.8	16.3
Panama	39.4	0.6	41.5	44.7	50.2	0.6	1.8	0.36	1.44	0.52	0.92	20	80	29	51	35.8	62.8
Paraguay	42.4	0.6	46.8	55.1	67.2	0.7	2.8	0.50	2.26	0.92	1.34	18	82	33	49	31.4	72.7
Peru	38.1	0.4	42.0	43.0	42.6	0.3	0.4	0.38	0.06	0.10	−0.04	86	14	23	−9	36.8	43.5
Uruguay	85.4	0.2	89.1	89.0	89.3	0.2	2.0	1.87	0.09	−0.08	0.17	95	5	−4	9	63.9	93.2
Venezuela, R. B.	87.6	0.3	94.0	92.6	88.1	0.2	0.0	0.63	−0.59	−0.14	−0.45	1,413	−1,313	−306	−1,007	87.6	88.3
LAC average	51.5		53.4	56.8	62.1		1.2	0.3	0.9	0.3	0.6	23.0	77.0	29.0	48.0	48.2	65.6

Source: Authors' calculations based on household surveys.

Table A2.4c HOI for Electricity and Decomposition (1995 and 2010)

Country	Opportunity index (%)							Decomposition (percentage points)				Decomposition (%)				Extrapolation (%)	
	Circa 1995		If the population of 2010 lived in 1995	Considering the inequality of 2010 and the average probability of 1995	Circa 2010		Annual rate of change (percentage points)	Composition effect	Coverage effect			Composition effect	Coverage effect			1995	2010
	Value	Standard error			Value	Standard error			Total	Equalization effect	Scale effect		Total	Equalization effect	Scale effect		
Argentina	99.1	0.1	—	—	100.0	0.0	0.1	—	—	—	—	—	—	—	—	98.8	100.0
Brazil	81.2	0.1	89.0	92.2	96.4	0.1	1.2	0.60	0.57	0.25	0.32	51	49	21	28	81.2	98.7
Chile	92.1	0.2	96.2	97.6	99.2	0.0	0.7	0.41	0.30	0.14	0.16	58	42	19	23	91.4	102.1
Colombia	86.0	0.3	95.1	97.0	100.0	0.1	1.2	0.83	0.39	0.17	0.21	68	32	14	17	83.6	102.4
Costa Rica	91.1	0.3	94.3	96.0	98.8	0.1	0.5	0.21	0.30	0.11	0.19	41	59	21	37	91.7	99.4
Dominican Republic	83.6	0.5	86.5	89.8	95.4	0.2	1.5	0.37	1.11	0.41	0.70	25	75	28	48	76.2	98.4
Ecuador	81.2	0.4	37.3	60.0	90.9	0.2	0.9	-3.99	4.87	2.06	2.81	-452	552	234	318	81.2	94.4
El Salvador	66.1	0.4	54.9	65.7	83.0	0.3	1.9	-1.25	3.12	1.20	1.92	-67	167	64	103	60.5	88.6
Guatemala	58.0	0.5	61.8	64.4	68.2	0.4	1.7	0.62	1.08	0.44	0.64	36	64	26	37	49.5	75.0
Honduras	48.4	0.5	48.1	50.2	53.2	0.3	0.7	-0.04	0.73	0.30	0.43	-6	106	44	62	45.7	55.9
Jamaica	74.2	1.0	72.9	75.0	85.4	0.5	1.9	-0.22	2.07	0.34	1.73	-12	112	18	93	72.4	100.0
Mexico	90.4	0.3	94.8	96.2	98.3	0.1	0.7	0.36	0.29	0.12	0.17	56	44	18	26	89.8	99.6
Nicaragua	48.7	0.7	45.7	47.6	52.5	0.5	0.5	-0.43	0.97	0.27	0.70	-80	180	50	130	47.1	55.2
Panama	55.0	0.5	60.6	60.9	60.2	0.5	0.9	0.94	-0.06	0.04	-0.10	107	-7	5	-12	53.2	66.4
Paraguay	83.6	0.5	86.7	89.2	94.7	0.4	1.2	0.34	0.89	0.28	0.61	28	72	23	50	78.7	97.1
Peru	47.7	0.4	52.3	57.7	64.4	0.3	1.7	0.46	1.21	0.54	0.67	27	73	32	40	42.8	67.7
Uruguay	97.6	0.1	98.2	98.2	98.2	0.1	0.3	0.31	-0.02	-0.03	0.02	105	-5	-11	6	94.3	98.8
Venezuela, R. B.	98.1	0.1	99.0	98.8	98.5	0.1	0.0	0.09	-0.05	-0.02	-0.03	210	-110	-42	-67	98.1	98.7
LAC average	76.8		74.9	78.6	85.4		1.0	0.0	1.0	0.4	0.7	-2.0	108.0	40.0	68.0	74.2	88.8

Source: Authors' calculations based on household surveys.

Note: — = data not available.

Table A2.4d HOI for Sanitation and Decomposition (1995 and 2010)

Country	Opportunity index (%)							Decomposition (percentage points)				Decomposition (%)				Extrapolation (%)	
	Circa 1995		If the population of 2010 lived in 1995	Considering the inequality of 2010 and the average probability of 1995	Circa 2010		Annual rate of change (percentage points)	Composition effect	Coverage effect			Composition effect	Coverage effect			1995	2010
	Value	Standard error	1995		Value	Standard error			Total	Equalization effect	Scale effect		Total	Equalization effect	Scale effect		
Argentina	54.3	0.5	66.1	66.2	64.4	0.5	1.0	1.19	-0.17	0.00	-0.17	117	-17	0	-17	51.2	66.5
Brazil	38.2	0.1	53.5	60.3	78.2	0.2	3.1	1.18	1.90	0.53	1.38	38	62	17	45	38.2	84.4
Chile	66.5	0.3	76.5	80.2	86.1	0.2	2.0	1.00	0.96	0.36	0.60	51	49	18	30	64.5	94.0
Colombia	64.0	0.4	68.0	72.6	77.0	0.4	1.2	0.36	0.83	0.42	0.41	30	70	35	34	61.6	79.4
Costa Rica	69.4	0.4	78.2	83.2	92.8	0.2	1.6	0.59	0.97	0.33	0.64	38	62	21	41	70.9	94.4
Dominican Republic	37.2	0.5	38.8	41.7	48.8	0.5	1.4	0.19	1.25	0.37	0.88	13	87	25	61	30.0	51.6
Ecuador	40.5	0.5	6.3	21.6	50.9	0.4	1.0	-3.11	4.06	1.39	2.67	-327	427	146	281	40.5	54.8
El Salvador	16.5	0.2	7.7	10.3	18.6	0.3	0.2	-0.98	1.21	0.28	0.93	-421	521	122	399	15.8	19.3
Guatemala	11.9	0.3	16.0	18.0	21.1	0.3	1.5	0.68	0.85	0.32	0.53	45	55	21	34	4.2	27.3
Honduras	32.1	0.4	30.7	27.9	25.6	0.2	-0.9	-0.20	-0.73	-0.41	-0.32	21	79	44	34	35.9	21.9
Jamaica	33.1	1.0	33.0	33.3	35.7	0.7	0.4	-0.03	0.45	0.06	0.39	-6	106	14	93	32.7	39.1
Mexico	46.1	0.4	67.5	67.6	72.0	0.3	2.2	1.79	0.38	0.00	0.37	83	17	0	17	43.9	76.3
Nicaragua	4.9	0.2	4.3	21.2	36.5	0.5	4.5	-0.08	4.60	2.41	2.19	-2	102	53	48	-8.7	59.1
Panama	29.3	0.4	33.4	33.2	31.4	0.5	0.3	0.69	-0.34	-0.04	-0.30	198	-98	-11	-86	28.6	33.8
Paraguay	35.7	0.5	39.3	41.8	48.4	0.6	1.4	0.40	1.01	0.27	0.74	28	72	19	52	30.1	51.2
Peru	31.3	0.4	35.4	44.3	54.4	0.3	2.3	0.41	1.91	0.90	1.01	18	82	39	44	24.3	59.0
Uruguay	96.3	0.1	97.4	97.2	96.6	0.1	0.1	0.56	-0.42	-0.13	-0.29	411	-311	-95	-215	94.8	96.8
Venezuela, R. B.	78.2	0.4	83.9	83.8	83.7	0.2	0.5	0.57	-0.02	-0.01	-0.01	104	-4	-2	-2	78.2	86.4
LAC average	43.6		46.5	50.2	56.8		1.3	0.3	1.0	0.4	0.6	22.0	78.0	30.0	49.0	40.9	60.9

Source: Authors' calculations based on household surveys.

Table A2.5 D-Index for Completing Sixth Grade on Time, by Circumstance, circa 2008

percent

Country	Parent's education	Gender	Gender of household head	Per capita income	Urban or rural	Presence of parents	Number of siblings	Overall D-index
Argentina	2.0	1.5	0.4	0.9	—	0.3	1.3	3.9
Bolivia	4.2	0.7	2.5	1.1	0.7	3.0	2.2	6.4
Brazil	11.3	9.5	0.4	8.9	2.0	2.7	3.2	19.1
Chile	1.7	0.9	1.0	0.8	0.0	0.2	1.5	3.0
Colombia	5.9	4.1	1.4	2.5	2.2	2.2	1.8	9.8
Costa Rica	5.4	2.6	1.5	0.7	1.0	1.9	3.8	7.7
Dominican Republic	9.9	6.7	0.8	4.6	0.8	0.4	3.4	13.5
Ecuador	3.5	0.3	0.3	1.6	0.1	0.1	1.6	5.9
El Salvador	10.1	3.6	2.5	4.3	4.4	0.3	4.7	15.9
Guatemala	20.5	2.8	8.4	5.3	9.2	6.0	7.0	26.6
Honduras	10.2	4.0	1.2	3.7	3.9	1.4	3.5	15.5
Jamaica	0.0	0.3	0.0	0.2	0.0	0.3	0.6	0.8
Mexico	2.1	1.0	0.6	0.4	0.4	0.6	1.0	3.4
Nicaragua	15.2	8.3	2.0	7.1	12.0	0.1	8.6	24.2
Panama	4.3	3.0	0.6	2.5	1.3	0.4	3.3	8.7
Paraguay	6.3	3.9	0.3	3.0	0.9	1.7	3.7	10.4
Peru	4.5	0.6	0.5	2.1	1.0	0.6	1.9	7.3
Uruguay	2.9	1.7	0.1	1.2	0.3	0.8	2.1	5.6
Venezuela, R. B.	3.7	2.4	0.1	0.8	0.4	0.4	2.5	6.1
LAC average	6.5	3.0	1.3	2.7	2.3	1.2	3.0	10.2

Source: Authors' calculations based on household surveys.

Note: — = data not available.

Table A2.6 D-Index for School Enrollment, by Circumstance, circa 2008

percent

Country	Parent's education	Gender	Gender of household head	Per capita income	Urban or rural	Presence of parents	Number of siblings	Overall D-index
Argentina	0.6	0.2	0.0	0.1	—	0.0	0.1	0.6
Bolivia	0.1	0.2	0.3	0.1	0.4	1.2	0.0	0.7
Brazil	0.3	0.1	0.2	0.1	0.0	0.1	0.0	0.4
Chile	0.2	0.0	0.1	0.2	0.0	0.1	0.0	0.4
Colombia	1.4	0.6	0.2	0.0	0.8	0.3	0.1	2.1
Costa Rica	0.9	0.1	0.1	0.0	0.3	0.3	0.0	1.1
Dominican Republic	0.6	0.2	0.1	0.0	0.1	0.2	0.0	0.6
Ecuador	2.2	0.2	0.2	0.6	0.9	0.0	0.2	3.3
El Salvador	1.8	0.3	0.7	0.6	0.4	0.5	0.5	2.7
Guatemala	3.8	1.4	2.1	1.1	1.0	2.8	0.2	4.8
Honduras	2.6	0.2	0.7	0.9	1.4	0.5	0.0	4.1
Jamaica	0.0	0.1	0.4	0.4	0.2	0.7	0.0	0.6
Mexico	1.4	0.2	0.2	0.1	0.2	0.2	0.3	1.9
Nicaragua	3.0	1.0	0.1	0.2	0.9	0.4	0.7	3.8
Panama	0.7	0.6	0.1	1.4	0.2	0.4	0.3	3.0
Paraguay	1.1	0.2	0.2	0.5	0.3	0.3	0.4	1.9
Peru	0.9	0.1	0.1	0.1	0.2	0.1	0.3	1.3
Uruguay	0.7	0.3	0.1	0.3	0.2	0.0	0.1	1.2
Venezuela, R. B.	0.8	0.5	0.1	0.1	0.1	0.2	0.3	1.3
LAC average	1.2	0.3	0.3	0.4	0.4	0.4	0.2	1.9

Source: Authors' calculations based on household surveys.

Note: — = data not available.

Table A2.7　D-Index for Sanitation, by Circumstance, circa 2008

percent

Country	Parent's education	Gender	Gender of household head	Per capita income	Urban or rural	Presence of parents	Number of siblings	Overall D-index
Argentina	6.5	0.3	0.1	6.1	—	0.6	1.3	11.3
Bolivia	15.1	0.6	6.2	10.1	27.8	0.8	4.6	32.0
Brazil	1.9	0.0	0.3	2.3	4.4	0.1	0.3	8.4
Chile	1.8	0.2	0.2	2.5	4.1	0.2	0.1	5.3
Colombia	3.2	0.1	0.5	2.7	4.0	0.3	0.6	8.0
Costa Rica	0.8	0.0	0.2	1.0	0.6	0.3	0.2	2.4
Dominican Republic	11.2	0.1	2.3	9.2	15.3	2.2	2.5	20.1
Ecuador	7.0	0.0	0.2	10.2	12.0	0.7	3.3	20.0
El Salvador	18.3	0.1	7.2	27.0	34.1	0.5	3.0	40.7
Guatemala	18.0	0.7	8.9	19.0	34.2	3.7	4.4	39.9
Honduras	13.6	0.3	1.3	17.3	23.5	1.8	0.4	34.3
Jamaica	3.1	1.3	7.7	2.6	20.5	7.1	5.2	21.0
Mexico	2.7	0.0	0.6	2.4	6.9	0.3	1.1	12.6
Nicaragua	8.2	0.5	2.0	7.6	12.9	0.4	1.4	20.0
Panama	14.6	1.1	1.3	20.1	21.1	4.4	3.1	31.2
Paraguay	8.5	0.1	1.4	10.9	15.2	0.3	2.0	22.4
Peru	4.8	0.1	0.5	4.4	11.1	0.3	0.7	16.2
Uruguay	0.3	0.0	0.1	0.6	0.1	0.0	0.0	1.1
Venezuela, R. B.	2.7	0.0	0.4	1.2	1.3	0.8	0.6	4.9
LAC average	7.5	0.3	2.2	8.3	13.8	1.3	1.8	18.5

Source: Authors' calculations based on household surveys.

Note: — = data not available.

Table A2.8 D-Index for Water, by Circumstance, circa 2008

percent

Country	Parent's education	Gender	Gender of household head	Per capita income	Urban or rural	Presence of parents	Number of siblings	Overall D-index
Argentina	0.4	0.0	0.1	0.2	—	0.0	0.1	0.8
Bolivia	2.3	0.4	0.1	1.2	11.7	0.2	1.0	14.2
Brazil	1.3	0.0	0.3	1.5	3.1	0.1	0.2	6.9
Chile	0.4	0.0	0.1	0.4	2.1	0.0	0.1	2.6
Colombia	6.0	0.3	2.7	8.3	11.7	0.3	3.9	17.6
Costa Rica	0.4	0.1	0.5	0.7	0.3	0.5	0.1	1.3
Dominican Republic	4.4	0.3	0.5	3.1	6.0	0.9	0.4	8.9
Ecuador	2.8	0.3	0.7	5.2	4.3	0.6	0.2	9.7
El Salvador	17.0	0.6	7.3	28.7	35.2	0.8	2.3	41.4
Guatemala	1.8	0.1	1.5	2.5	8.0	0.9	0.3	9.8
Honduras	15.4	0.8	1.5	16.2	15.4	0.4	1.9	32.0
Jamaica	6.7	1.1	8.0	2.3	29.2	5.1	6.9	29.5
Mexico	1.3	0.2	0.5	1.3	3.7	0.1	0.7	5.9
Nicaragua	13.6	3.0	3.4	19.0	35.2	4.8	4.1	41.1
Panama	5.7	0.4	0.8	12.2	7.2	1.5	0.4	17.1
Paraguay	3.5	0.2	1.2	4.4	4.5	1.0	0.6	9.2
Peru	3.4	0.1	0.6	8.0	15.2	0.1	1.3	20.8
Uruguay	0.8	0.0	0.1	1.8	0.8	0.0	0.1	3.8
Venezuela, R. B.	1.4	0.0	0.0	0.5	1.9	0.6	0.1	3.2
LAC average	4.7	0.4	1.6	6.2	10.9	0.9	1.3	14.5

Source: Authors' calculations based on household surveys.

Note: — = data not available.

Table A2.9 D-Index for Electricity, by Circumstance, circa 2008

percent

Country	Parent's education	Gender	Gender of household head	Per capita income	Urban or rural	Presence of parents	Number of siblings	Overall D-index
Argentina	—	—	—	—	—	—	—	—
Bolivia	2.6	0.1	1.0	1.4	9.6	0.2	0.4	15.9
Brazil	0.1	0.0	0.0	0.1	0.5	0.0	0.0	1.6
Chile	0.1	0.0	0.0	0.1	0.1	0.0	0.0	0.3
Colombia	0.0	0.0	0.1	0.1	0.0	0.0	0.0	0.1
Costa Rica	0.1	0.0	0.0	0.1	0.1	0.0	0.0	0.4
Dominican Republic	0.4	0.0	0.1	0.1	0.8	0.0	0.0	1.8
Ecuador	0.2	0.0	0.1	0.7	1.6	0.0	0.3	3.6
El Salvador	1.5	0.1	0.2	1.8	2.8	0.0	0.4	6.2
Guatemala	4.2	0.1	1.7	4.5	4.6	0.1	0.7	10.1
Honduras	3.3	0.1	0.6	6.6	11.5	0.0	0.4	20.7
Jamaica	0.8	0.1	1.3	0.5	1.8	0.6	0.3	2.5
Mexico	0.1	0.0	0.0	0.0	0.3	0.1	0.1	0.6
Nicaragua	6.7	0.6	2.6	5.6	15.7	0.1	0.9	21.5
Panama	3.2	0.4	1.0	9.4	9.0	0.1	3.2	18.3
Paraguay	0.3	0.1	0.1	0.6	0.7	0.0	0.1	1.8
Peru	3.5	0.1	0.1	1.8	10.4	0.1	1.0	15.5
Uruguay	0.1	0.0	0.0	0.1	0.3	0.0	0.0	0.7
Venezuela, R. B.	0.1	0.0	0.0	0.1	0.3	0.0	0.0	0.5
LAC average	1.5	0.1	0.5	1.9	3.9	0.1	0.4	6.8

Source: Authors' calculations based on household surveys.

Note: — = data not available.

Table A2.10 Decomposition of Coverage Effect in Components of Education HOI

percent

| | Finished sixth grade on time | | | | | | | | | School attendance (ages 10–14) | | | | | | | | |
| | Percentage points | | | | | Percent | | | | Percentage points | | | | | Percent | | | |
Country	Total change	Composition effect	Total coverage effect	Equalization effect	Scale effect	Composition effect	Total coverage effect	Equalization effect	Scale effect	Total change	Composition effect	Total coverage effect	Equalization effect	Scale effect	Composition effect	Total coverage effect	Equalization effect	Scale effect
Argentina	-0.2	0.3	-0.4	-0.1	-0.4	-160	260	32	228	0.0	0.1	-0.1	0.0	-0.1	-248	348	-6	354
Brazil	1.5	0.4	1.1	0.4	0.7	28	72	25	47	0.8	0.3	0.5	0.2	0.4	33	67	21	46
Chile	0.8	0.5	0.4	0.1	0.2	57	43	14	29	0.1	0.1	0.0	0.0	0.0	72	28	8	20
Colombia	1.9	0.4	1.4	0.6	0.8	21	74	32	42	0.7	0.2	0.4	0.1	0.3	29	57	14	43
Costa Rica	0.6	0.5	0.1	0.0	0.0	90	10	2	7	0.7	0.3	0.5	0.1	0.4	34	66	16	51
Dominican Republic	1.9	0.4	1.5	0.4	1.0	22	78	22	55	-0.1	0.0	-0.1	0.0	-0.1	9	91	-32	123
Ecuador	1.3	-0.8	2.2	0.6	1.6	-63	163	46	117	0.6	0.5	0.1	0.0	0.0	85	15	7	8
El Salvador	1.6	-0.5	2.1	0.6	1.5	-34	134	38	95	0.9	-0.4	1.3	0.3	1.0	-42	142	32	110
Guatemala	1.3	0.4	0.9	0.5	0.4	34	66	35	31	1.1	0.2	0.9	0.1	0.7	21	79	13	65
Honduras	1.7	0.2	1.5	0.3	1.2	12	88	19	69	1.3	-0.1	1.4	0.3	1.1	-8	108	26	82
Jamaica	0.5	0.1	0.4	0.1	0.4	21	79	11	67	0.1	0.0	0.1	0.0	0.1	-26	126	30	96
Mexico	1.7	0.9	0.7	0.2	0.5	56	44	14	31	0.6	0.4	0.2	0.1	0.1	69	31	10	20
Nicaragua	1.5	0.1	1.4	0.3	1.1	8	92	17	74	1.2	-0.1	1.4	0.4	1.0	-11	111	31	79
Panama	0.5	0.6	-0.1	0.0	-0.2	128	-28	9	-37	0.3	0.3	0.1	0.0	0.1	83	17	-3	20
Paraguay	1.2	0.6	0.6	0.2	0.5	47	53	14	38	0.1	0.1	0.0	0.0	0.0	102	-2	8	-10
Peru	2.2	0.6	1.7	0.5	1.2	25	75	22	53	0.3	0.2	0.1	0.1	0.1	51	49	19	30
Uruguay	1.4	0.5	0.9	0.2	0.7	38	62	13	50	-0.4	0.2	-0.7	-0.2	-0.5	-56	156	35	121
Venezuela, R.B.	1.1	0.7	0.4	0.1	0.3	60	40	11	28	0.3	0.2	0.1	0.0	0.1	70	30	6	24
LAC average	1.3	0.3	0.9	0.3	0.6	26	74	22	51	0.5	0.1	0.3	0.1	0.3	27	73	19	53

Source: Authors' calculations based on household surveys.

Table A2.11 Decomposition of Coverage Effect in Components of Housing HOI

percent

	Water								
	Percentage points					*Percent*			
Country	*Total change*	*Composition effect*	*Total coverage effect*	*Equalization effect*	*Scale effect*	*Composition effect*	*Total coverage effect*	*Equalization effect*	*Scale effect*
Argentina	0.2	0.2	0.0	0.0	0.0	80.2	19.8	6.2	13.6
Brazil	1.6	0.9	0.7	0.3	0.4	56.4	43.6	16.5	27.1
Chile	1.1	0.7	0.4	0.2	0.2	61.7	38.3	17.1	21.2
Colombia	-0.2	0.3	-0.6	0.0	-0.5	-150.0	300.0	0.0	250.0
Costa Rica	0.2	0.0	0.2	0.0	0.2	16.1	83.9	3.7	80.2
Dominican Republic	0.9	0.3	0.6	0.2	0.4	35.9	64.1	19.7	44.4
Ecuador	4.1	-2.0	6.0	2.6	3.5	-48.8	148.8	62.8	86.0
El Salvador	0.0	-1.0	1.0	0.1	0.9	-4,190.1	4,290.1	359.1	3,931.0
Guatemala	1.4	0.5	0.9	0.3	0.6	34.6	65.4	19.6	45.8
Honduras	0.9	0.0	0.9	0.4	0.6	1.5	98.5	39.5	59.0
Jamaica	-0.6	-0.1	-0.5	-0.2	-0.3	21.6	78.4	25.5	52.9
Mexico	4.0	1.4	2.6	1.0	1.6	35.2	64.8	24.7	40.1
Nicaragua	0.3	-0.2	0.5	0.1	0.4	-54.6	154.6	28.4	126.3
Panama	1.8	0.4	1.4	0.5	0.9	20.0	80.0	29.0	51.0
Paraguay	2.8	0.5	2.3	0.9	1.3	18.0	82.0	33.4	48.6
Peru	0.4	0.4	0.1	0.1	0.0	85.8	14.2	23.5	-9.3
Uruguay	2.0	1.9	0.1	-0.1	0.2	95.4	4.6	-4.0	8.6
Venezuela, R. B.	0.0	0.6	-0.6	-0.1	-0.5	1,412.7	-1,312.7	-306.1	-1,006.6
LAC average	1.2	0.3	0.9	0.3	0.6	23	77	29	48

(continued next page)

Table A2.11 (continued)

	Sanitation								
	Percentage points					Percent			
			Total				Total		
Country	Total change	Composition effect	coverage effect	Equalization effect	Scale effect	Composition effect	coverage effect	Equalization effect	Scale effect
Argentina	1.0	1.2	-0.2	0.0	-0.2	116.6	-16.6	0.5	-17.0
Brazil	3.1	1.2	1.9	0.5	1.4	38.2	61.8	17.1	44.7
Chile	2.0	1.0	1.0	0.4	0.6	51.2	48.8	18.5	30.4
Colombia	1.2	0.4	0.8	0.4	0.4	33.3	66.7	33.3	33.3
Costa Rica	1.6	0.6	1.0	0.3	0.6	37.7	62.3	21.3	41.0
Dominican Republic	1.4	0.2	1.2	0.4	0.9	13.3	86.7	25.4	61.3
Ecuador	1.0	-3.1	4.1	1.4	2.7	-326.7	426.7	146.1	280.6
El Salvador	0.2	-1.0	1.2	0.3	0.9	-421.1	521.1	122.0	399.1
Guatemala	1.5	0.7	0.9	0.3	0.5	44.5	55.5	21.0	34.4
Honduras	-0.9	-0.2	-0.7	-0.4	-0.3	21.4	78.6	44.1	34.5
Jamaica	0.4	0.0	0.5	0.1	0.4	-6.5	106.5	13.9	92.6
Mexico	2.2	1.8	0.4	0.0	0.4	82.6	17.4	0.2	17.2
Nicaragua	4.5	-0.1	4.6	2.4	2.2	-1.7	101.7	53.3	48.5
Panama	0.3	0.7	-0.3	0.0	-0.3	197.7	-97.7	-11.3	-86.5
Paraguay	1.4	0.4	1.0	0.3	0.7	28.4	71.6	19.3	52.3
Peru	2.3	0.4	1.9	0.9	1.0	17.6	82.4	38.8	43.6
Uruguay	0.1	0.6	-0.4	-0.1	-0.3	410.7	-310.7	-95.3	-215.4
Venezuela, R. B.	0.5	0.6	0.0	0.0	0.0	104.1	-4.1	-2.1	-2.0
LAC average	1.3	0.3	1.0	0.4	0.6	22.0	78.0	29.0	49.0

Country	Electricity					Percent			
	Percentage points								
	Total change	Composition effect	Total coverage effect	Equalization effect	Scale effect	Composition effect	Total coverage effect	Equalization effect	Scale effect
Argentina	—	—	—	—	—	—	—	—	—
Brazil	1.2	0.6	0.6	0.2	0.3	51.2	48.8	21.1	27.7
Chile	0.7	0.4	0.3	0.1	0.2	57.9	42.1	19.1	23.0
Colombia	1.2	0.8	0.4	0.2	0.2	66.7	33.3	16.7	16.7
Costa Rica	0.5	0.2	0.3	0.1	0.2	41.3	58.7	21.5	37.3
Dominican Republic	1.5	0.4	1.1	0.4	0.7	24.8	75.2	27.5	47.7
Ecuador	0.9	-4.0	4.9	2.1	2.8	-452.3	552.3	233.9	318.4
El Salvador	1.9	-1.3	3.1	1.2	1.9	-67.0	167.0	64.3	102.6
Guatemala	1.7	0.6	1.1	0.4	0.6	36.5	63.5	26.1	37.4
Honduras	0.7	0.0	0.7	0.3	0.4	-6.3	106.3	43.9	62.3
Jamaica	1.9	-0.2	2.1	0.3	1.7	-11.7	111.7	18.4	93.2
Mexico	0.7	0.4	0.3	0.1	0.2	55.9	44.1	18.0	26.1
Nicaragua	0.5	-0.4	1.0	0.3	0.7	-79.6	179.6	49.7	129.9
Panama	0.9	0.9	-0.1	0.0	-0.1	107.0	-7.0	4.9	-11.8
Paraguay	1.2	0.3	0.9	0.3	0.6	27.9	72.1	22.5	49.6
Peru	1.7	0.5	1.2	0.5	0.7	27.4	72.6	32.4	40.2
Uruguay	0.3	0.3	0.0	0.0	0.0	105.1	-5.1	-11.4	6.3
Venezuela, R. B.	0.0	0.1	0.0	0.0	0.0	209.5	-109.5	-42.4	-67.2
LAC average	1.0	0.0	1.0	0.4	0.7	-2	102.0	38.0	64.0

Source: Authors' calculations based on household surveys.
Note: — = data not available.

Notes

1. Bolivia is an exception, for which only one year of data was used. Consequently, estimates of rates of change or of extrapolated values and future projections were not possible for Bolivia. In addition, the varying dates of surveys used for the HOI pose serious comparison challenges. To reduce this comparability problem, we use the two point estimates to extrapolate forward and obtain an estimate for 2010 overall HOI, given the recent level and pace of change of the overall HOI for each particular country in the sample. This adjustment permits us to assess countries at a similar point in time.

2. Assuming a linear expansion, we estimate the year of achieving universal coverage by (100 − current HOI) / annual rate of growth. The results are essentially the same if we assume that "universality" is achieved with a coverage rate of 98 percent. With this latter assumption it will take 22 years instead of 24 to universalize the basic services contained in the HOI. The linearity assumption can be also seen as optimistic. If we consider that there is a slowing in the pace of progress as the HOI approaches universality, as the evidence suggests (see chapters 3 and 4), it will take much longer to universalize the set of basic services considered.

3. Changes in circumstances would not expand a child's opportunities in a society with completely equal opportunity, because all circumstance groups would have the same opportunities. However, in the context of significant inequality of opportunity, policies aimed at improving certain circumstances, such as family income or parents' education, may be instrumental in expanding a child's access to basic goods and services.

4. For more details, see annex tables A2.2 to A2.4.

5. The equality of opportunity measure D is used to estimate the penalty that discounts the overall coverage rate. As discussed in chapter 1, the penalty is the product of the inequality of opportunity measure and the overall coverage rate ($P = C \times D$).

Bibliography

Azevedo, J. P., S. Franco, Eliana Rubiano, and Alejandro Hoyos. 2010. "HOI: Stata Module to Compute Human Opportunity Index." Statistical Software Components S457191, version 1.7. Boston College Department of Economics. http://ideas.repec.org/c/boc/bocode/s457191.html.

CHAPTER 3

Human Opportunities in a Global Context: Benchmarking LAC to Other Regions of the World

The previous chapter showed that the Latin America and the Caribbean (LAC) region has made progress in improving equality of opportunities for children to access basic goods and services, but that universality has not been achieved everywhere. To build consensus around the agenda ahead, in this chapter we compare Human Opportunity Indices (HOIs) in educational achievement and housing between LAC and other countries in North America and Europe. How much progress does LAC need to make to reach Organisation for Economic Co-operation and Development (OECD) minimum standards? What are the main sources of the differences between LAC and OECD countries? Are the observed differences similar across education and housing dimensions?

The chapter finds that, despite gains in recent years, the gap between LAC and OECD countries in Europe and North America remains large in both education and housing HOIs. Education quality outcomes were notably worse for LAC, with even the highest country scores falling below the lowest scores of Europe, Canada, and the United States. Much of the education HOI gap is attributed to inequality of opportunity levels, which are often two or three times higher in LAC than in European and North American countries. LAC fared somewhat better in housing indicators, with HOIs for access to sanitation and freedom from overcrowding exceeding the European average in two and three LAC countries, respectively. As with education, much of the housing HOI gap is attributed to inequality of opportunity levels, which are often twice as high in LAC as in European and North American countries.

In the case of two countries (United States and France), we exploit the availability of a long time series to draw some lessons on the evolution of the HOI over multiple decades that could be relevant to LAC. Analyzing the expansion of the HOI for housing opportunities in the United States and France from the 1960s indicates that HOI levels are initially low, experience fast growth rates, and then slow down as the HOI reaches a high level.

The chapter is organized as follows. Section 3.1 describes the data underlying the construction of the HOI for educational achievement and presents results. Section 3.2 describes the data used in constructing HOIs for access to sanitation and freedom from overcrowding and presents results. Section 3.3 describes how the HOI evolves over long time periods. Section 3.4 concludes.

HOI for Quality Education

Educational achievement measured by test scores better captures the true chances of children to meet the challenges of the future than educational attainment measured by years of schooling or even completion on time, because of considerable heterogeneity in the quality of education across schools. To some extent, educational achievement is a good proxy for the quality of schools. Therefore, to estimate the HOIs for quality education, we use data on educational achievement from the OECD's Programme for International Student Assessment (PISA).

Estimating the HOI for Quality Education

PISA is a triennial, internationally comparable survey of the knowledge and skills of 15-year-olds in reading, mathematics, and science. PISA assesses the degree to which students near the end of compulsory education can extrapolate from what they have learned and apply their knowledge in both school and nonschool contexts, thus giving an indication of how well they have gained the skills and knowledge needed for full participation in society (OECD 2007).

Reading literacy is measured in terms of students' abilities to use written information in situations that they encounter in their lives. Mathematical literacy measures students' abilities to pose, solve, and interpret mathematical problems in a variety of situations involving quantitative, spatial, probabilistic, or other mathematical concepts. Scientific literacy measures students' abilities to identify, explain and apply scientific knowledge and knowledge about science in a variety of complex life situations (box 3.1).

Students are placed in different proficiency levels according to the difficulty of tasks that they can complete. There are six proficiency levels for reading and seven levels for mathematics and science.[1] Proficiency level 2 is usually considered the level that requires the basic tasks students need to apply the subject area in real-life contexts. About 80 percent of students in OECD countries are at level 2 or above. Longitudinal follow-up studies in Australia, Canada, and Denmark find that the minority of students classified at either level 1 or below are very likely to face difficulties using reading materials to fulfill their goals and to acquire knowledge (OECD 2007: 46). The average for students in OECD countries is level 3.

For the HOI for quality education, we focus on whether a student achieves a minimum score to place him- or herself at proficiency level 2. Hence, the coverage rate of quality education used in the HOI is the proportion of students that took the test and achieved a score that placed the student at least at proficiency level 2.

PISA surveys contain information on a common set of six circumstances: gender of the child, father's and mother's education, school location, father's occupation, and household asset items that allow us to generate a wealth index (see table A3.1 for more details).

We compute the HOI for quality education by estimating a logistic model on whether student i had achieved at least proficiency level 2 as a function of his or her circumstances. Based on the predicted probabilities, we compute the coverage rate, the dissimilarity index, the penalty for inequality of opportunity, and the HOI, following the methodology described in chapter 1.

The HOIs for Reading Proficiency

The HOIs for reading proficiency in LAC countries are consistently lower than in European countries and Canada, according to findings from 16 countries from the 2006 round of PISA (table 3.2).[2] The HOIs for reading proficiency range from a high of 90 for Canada to a low of 37 for Argentina. Among the six Latin American countries included in PISA 2006, Chile performs best, with an HOI for reading of 59. However, even Chile is considerably below the lowest performing European country in the sample, Italy, with an HOI of 70.

Box 3.1

The PISA Data

The first PISA survey was conducted in 2000, and in 2006 the third survey included 30 OECD and 27 non-OECD countries. PISA surveys are administered in countries that together make up close to 90 percent of the world economy.[a]

The samples of students are nationally representative of the populations of 15-year-olds attending schools in grade 7 and above (table 3.1). In 2006 the samples used were representative of 20 million 15-year-olds. More than 400,000 students in 57 countries took a two-hour comparable test. Students also completed a questionnaire about themselves, and their principals completed a

Table 3.1   Sampling and Coverage Rates

Country	All 15-year-olds (a)	Enrolled 15 year-olds (b)	Ratio (b)/(a)	Target population (c)	Ratio (c)/(b)	Participants	Coverage index
Latin America							
Argentina	662,686	579,222	0.87	579,222	1.00	4,339	0.99
Brazil	3,390,471	2,374,044	0.70	2,357,355	0.99	9,295	0.99
Chile	299,426	255,459	0.85	255,393	1.00	5,235	0.99
Colombia	897,477	543,630	0.61	543,630	1.00	4,478	0.99
Mexico	2,200,916	1,383,364	0.63	1,383,364	1.00	30,971	1.00
Uruguay	52,119	40,815	0.78	40,815	1.00	4,839	1.00
Europe							
France	809,375	809,375	1.00	777,194	0.96	4,716	0.91
Germany	951,535	1,062,920	1.12	1,062,920	1.00	4,891	0.99
Italy	578,131	639,971	1.11	639,971	1.00	21,773	0.98
Norway	61,708	61,449	1.00	61,373	1.00	4,692	0.96
Portugal	115,426	100,816	0.87	100,816	1.00	5,109	0.98
Spain	439,415	436,885	0.99	436,885	1.00	19,604	0.96
Sweden	129,734	127,036	0.98	127,036	1.00	4,443	0.96
United Kingdom	779,076	767,248	0.98	767,248	1.00	13,252	0.97
North America							
Canada	426,967	428,876	1.00	424,238	0.99	22,646	0.93
United States	4,192,939	4,192,939	1.00	4,192,939	1.00	5,611	0.96

Source: Estimates based on PISA 2006 data (OECD 2007).

(continued next page)

Box 3.1 *(continued)*

questionnaire about their schools. The samples do not cover drop-outs and students attending grades below 7.

Although the enrollment of 15-year-olds is generally universal in Europe, it is not so in LAC. With the exception of Portugal, all European countries considered have enrollment rates of 98 percent and above for 15-year-olds. By contrast, the proportion of 15-year-olds enrolled in the school system is as low as 61 and 63 percent in Colombia and Mexico, respectively.[b] To the extent that 15-year-olds not enrolled in schools would not be able to achieve minimum expected knowledge, a low proportion of enrollment may overestimate a national measure of the educational achievement of 15-year-olds.

Source: OECD 2007.
a. In 2009, PISA was administered in 30 OECD countries and 37 non-OECD countries/economies. Hong Kong SAR, China is included.
b. The proportion of enrolled 15-year-olds that are below seventh grade (not targeted population) is negligible in all countries, except France.

Table 3.2   HOI for Reading Proficiency at Level 2

	Coverage	D-index	Penalty	HOI	Standard error
Latin America					
Argentina	47	20	9	37	0.9
Brazil	47	19	9	38	0.8
Colombia	48	15	7	41	1.2
Mexico	56	16	9	47	0.7
Uruguay	57	15	9	49	1.0
Chile	67	11	8	59	0.9
Europe					
Italy	76	8	6	70	0.5
Portugal	78	9	7	71	0.8
Spain	77	8	6	71	0.7
France	83	7	6	77	0.7
Norway	83	6	5	78	0.8
Germany	87	6	5	82	0.7
United Kingdom	87	5	4	83	0.6
Sweden	88	4	4	85	0.8
North America					
Canada	92	3	2	90	0.4
United States	—	—	—	—	—

Source: Estimates based on PISA data 2006 (OECD 2007).
Note: Canada and France do not include school location as a circumstance variable. Data for the United States not available.

The HOI discounts the coverage rate with a penalty that is proportional to the degree of inequality of opportunity in the allocation of existing basic services. The inequality of opportunity for acquiring adequate reading in LAC countries, as measured by the *D*-indices, is about twice the magnitude observed in European and North American countries (table 3.2). To reduce inequality of opportunity more effectively, policy makers need to know the inequality of opportunity profile for a given society to design effective public policies.

To build this profile, we report the specific *D*-indices that inform us about the inequality of opportunity associated with each specific circumstance (table 3.3). A profile of inequality of opportunity can be defined by the relative size of each *D*-index to a specific circumstance (socioeconomic status, gender, etc.).[3] These specific *D*-indices represent the percentage of the available opportunity for adequate reading ability that would have to be reallocated among children for equality of opportunity to prevail, if only one circumstance were considered. For instance, if we considered only gender of the child, roughly 12 percent of available opportunities for accessing adequate reading in Argentina would need to be reallocated, compared with 3.4 percent of available opportunities if we considered only father's education.

Overall, socioeconomic status is the most important circumstance associated with inequality of opportunity for reading in Canada, Latin America, and European countries. It is the most important circumstance in half the LAC countries considered as well as in half of the European countries considered. However, the weight of the circumstance is much higher in Latin America: Only 1.2 percent of the available opportunities for accessing quality reading would need to be reallocated in Canada for equality of opportunity to prevail if the only circumstance considered was socioeconomic status, compared with 10 percent in Argentina. Gender of the child is the second most important circumstance, and school location is also important in some LAC countries, notably Colombia and Mexico.

The HOIs for Mathematical Proficiency

The HOIs for mathematical proficiency in LAC countries are substantially lower than in European and North American countries (table 3.4). The HOIs for mathematics range from a high of 90 for Canada to a low of 20 for Brazil. Among the six Latin American countries included in PISA 2006, Uruguay is the best-performing country, with an HOI for mathematics proficiency at level 2 of 50. However, even Uruguay is considerably below the lowest performing European country in our sample, Italy (63),

Table 3.3 Profile of Inequality of Opportunity: Specific D-Indices for Proficiency at Level 2 in Reading

	Gender	School location	Father's education	Mother's education	Socioeconomic status	Father's occupation	Overall D-index
Latin America							
Argentina	11.9	5.7	3.4	4.0	9.6	9.0	19.8
Brazil	8.8	4.0	4.8	4.7	9.2	8.1	19.1
Chile	3.7	3.9	2.1	3.5	3.4	3.5	11.4
Colombia	3.0	5.5	3.6	3.8	7.2	4.6	15.0
Mexico	7.4	8.0	2.7	4.0	3.9	3.3	16.0
Uruguay	7.6	2.5	2.1	4.0	7.5	4.1	14.8
Europe							
France	2.1		0.5	1.1	3.7	2.8	7.1
Germany	1.9	1.0	0.9	1.7	2.1	2.0	6.0
Italy	4.4	2.8	1.5	1.6	3.9	2.4	7.7
Norway	3.7	0.4	0.6	0.7	2.6	3.2	5.9
Portugal	2.4	1.3	1.3	2.6	4.7	3.7	9.0
Spain	2.9	1.0	1.1	1.9	3.8	3.2	8.0
Sweden	2.4	0.3	1.2	0.5	1.9	1.8	4.2
United Kingdom	1.8	0.8	1.0	0.4	2.2	2.7	4.8
North America							
Canada	1.6	0.4	0.3	0.3	1.2	1.0	2.6

Source: Estimates based on PISA 2006 data (OECD 2007).

Table 3.4   HOI for Mathematics Proficiency at Level 2

	Coverage	D-index	Penalty	HOI	Standard error
Latin America					
Brazil	29	29	8	20	0.6
Colombia	30	25	7	22	0.9
Argentina	39	22	9	31	0.8
Chile	46	23	10	36	0.8
Mexico	45	18	8	37	0.6
Uruguay	58	14	8	50	1.0
Europe					
Italy	69	9	6	63	0.6
Portugal	72	10	7	65	0.8
Spain	78	7	5	72	0.7
France	83	7	6	77	0.7
Norway	82	5	4	78	0.8
Sweden	85	5	4	81	0.8
Germany	86	5	5	82	0.7
United Kingdom	86	5	4	82	0.6
North America					
United States	76	8	6	70	0.8
Canada	92	2	2	90	0.4

Source: Estimates based on PISA 2006 data (OECD 2007).
Note: Canada and France do not include school location as a circumstance variable.

as well as compared with the United States (70), the low performer in North America.

Socioeconomic status is the circumstance most strongly associated with inequality of opportunity for accessing quality education in mathematics in Latin America and Europe (table 3.5). It is the most important circumstance in four out of six LAC countries considered and in five out of eight European countries considered. Father's occupation is the second most important circumstance.

The HOIs for Science Proficiency

The HOIs for science proficiency in LAC countries are also substantially lower than in European and North American countries (table 3.6). Scores range from 91 for Canada to 33 for Brazil. Among the six Latin American countries included in PISA 2006, Chile and Uruguay are the best-performing countries with HOIs for science of 54. However, even Chile and Uruguay are considerably below the lowest performing European countries in our sample, Italy and Portugal, with HOIs of 71 and 72, respectively.

Socioeconomic status, again, is the circumstance most strongly associated with inequality of opportunity for accessing quality education in

Table 3.5 Profile of Inequality of Opportunity: Specific D-Indices for Proficiency at Level 2 in Mathematics

	Gender	School location	Father's education	Mother's education	Socioeconomic status	Father's occupation	Overall D-index
Latin America							
Argentina	3.9	7.2	5.2	5.1	12.5	8.1	22.2
Brazil	5.9	5.9	9.4	10.5	13.8	11.9	29.3
Chile	7.2	5.0	4.7	8.9	8.7	8.6	22.7
Colombia	10.8	5.4	5.8	5.7	13.3	10.0	24.7
Mexico	4.1	9.5	2.4	6.5	5.6	4.1	18.5
Uruguay	2.3	3.1	2.5	5.5	6.6	3.5	14.1
Europe							
France	0.8		1.5	1.7	3.8	2.9	7.0
Germany	1.1	0.9	0.8	1.7	2.4	2.2	5.4
Italy	2.7	2.7	1.0	1.7	5.2	3.4	8.5
Norway	0.7	0.8	0.8	0.8	2.6	3.3	4.9
Portugal	1.9	1.8	3.0	2.6	5.5	5.2	10.0
Spain	0.8	0.6	0.7	1.9	4.0	3.2	7.0
Sweden	0.4	0.4	1.5	0.8	1.9	3.1	4.7
United Kingdom	0.8	1.1	1.3	0.7	2.5	2.6	4.9
North America							
Canada	0.3	0.4	0.1	0.2	1.0	1.4	1.9
United States	0.8	3.0	0.5	1.4	2.4	4.9	7.8

Source: Estimates based on PISA 2006 data (OECD 2007).

Table 3.6   HOI for Science Proficiency at Level 2

	Coverage	D-index	Penalty	HOI	Standard error
Latin America					
Brazil	42	22	9	33	0.8
Colombia	43	16	7	37	1.1
Argentina	48	20	10	39	0.9
Mexico	52	17	9	43	0.7
Uruguay	62	13	8	54	1.0
Chile	63	13	8	54	0.9
Europe					
Italy	77	7	5	71	0.5
Portugal	78	8	6	72	0.8
France	84	7	6	78	0.7
Spain	83	6	5	78	0.6
Norway	84	5	4	80	0.7
Sweden	87	4	3	84	0.8
United Kingdom	89	4	4	85	0.6
Germany	90	4	4	86	0.7
North America					
United States	80	7	6	74	0.8
Canada	93	2	2	91	0.4

Source: Estimates based on PISA 2006 data (OECD 2007).
Note: Canada and France do not include school location as a circumstance variable.

science in Latin America (table 3.7). It is the most important circumstance in five out of six LAC countries considered. Father's occupation is the second most important circumstance.

The HOI for Housing

In this section we examine how LAC countries compare with other regions around the world on access to sanitation and the degree of overcrowding within the home. Although the importance of access to sanitation has been underscored in chapter 1, the importance of overcrowded housing bears discussion here.

Evidence on the negative impact of overcrowding has been compiled in numerous studies around the world. This ranges from evidence on the link between mental health and overcrowding in Thailand (Fuller and others 1993) to evidence that relationships between parents and children suffer in overcrowded settings in the United States (Gove, Hughes, and Galle 1979). Studies have examined the link between overcrowding and the likelihood of being exposed to unhygienic conditions and the causal link between overcrowding and educational attainment and progress

Table 3.7 Profile of Inequality of Opportunity: Specific D-Indices for Proficiency at Level 2 in Science

	Gender	School location	Father's education	Mother's education	Socioeconomic status	Father's occupation	Overall D-index
Latin America							
Argentina	2.9	6.2	4.1	5.8	10.8	7.5	21.5
Brazil	2.0	5.2	4.0	7.8	10.6	10.0	15.6
Chile	2.6	3.0	3.2	4.6	4.6	3.5	19.7
Colombia	4.0	4.5	2.9	4.0	7.7	6.4	16.6
Mexico	2.0	9.3	2.4	4.7	4.9	4.1	13.0
Uruguay	1.7	2.3	3.5	3.4	6.5	3.3	13.3
Europe							
France	0.3		1.0	1.4	3.7	2.8	7.0
Germany	0.4	0.8	0.6	1.3	1.4	1.9	8.0
Italy	0.1	2.3	1.5	1.4	4.1	2.6	6.9
Norway	0.3	1.2	0.3	0.7	2.6	2.8	5.8
Portugal	0.6	0.7	1.7	2.3	4.3	4.1	4.6
Spain	0.6	0.6	0.7	1.7	3.1	2.3	3.8
Sweden	0.3	0.4	1.3	0.8	1.6	2.5	4.1
United Kingdom	0.1	0.7	1.0	0.6	2.1	2.2	4.3
North America							
Canada	0.2	0.5	0.6	0.2	1.0	1.2	7.2
United States	0.7	3.0	0.5	1.0	2.6	4.1	2.0

Source: Estimates based on PISA 2006 data.

(Coggan and others 1993; Currie and Yelowitz 2000; Goux and Maurin 2005). This confluence of evidence has led some countries to develop statutory overcrowding standards (United Kingdom) and others to develop targeting indicators to monitor the proportion of households living in overcrowded conditions (United States). Because of the growing awareness of its importance, this study compares freedom from severe overcrowding among different countries.

The Data

For non-LAC countries, we use census micro-samples from the Integrated Public Use Microdata Series (IPUMS) International databases. The IPUMS data contain information on access to sanitation services. Data also include the gender of the child, the gender of the head of the household, urban or rural residence, number of siblings, whether the child lives with both parents, and the completed education level of the head of the household. Because total household income was not comparable across samples, this circumstance variable was excluded.[4] Because these are samples of the census data, all calculations were weighted (see table A3.3a for more details). For LAC countries, we use the harmonized household surveys from the SEDLAC database described in chapter 2.

Severe overcrowding is generally considered to exist when there are more than 1.5 people per room on average (although the United States considers overcrowding any level above one person per room). By combining IPUMS data on number of rooms with information on the number of people in the household, we derive the number of people per room to use in the overcrowding HOI.

The HOI for Sanitation

When only access to a public sanitation connection is considered, the majority of LAC countries we analyzed were below the average for all available European countries of approximately 55 (figure 3.1). Only two LAC countries, República Bolivariana de Venezuela (81) and Chile (74), report HOI levels substantially above the European average. The HOI for Mexico is only marginally above the European average (56). When the definition is broadened to include septic tanks, eight countries are above the European average of 70 (figure 3.2). The remaining countries also improve when considering septic systems but remain below the average of the European countries.[5] Much of the sanitation HOI gap is attributed

Figure 3.1   HOI Access to Sanitation, Public Connection Only

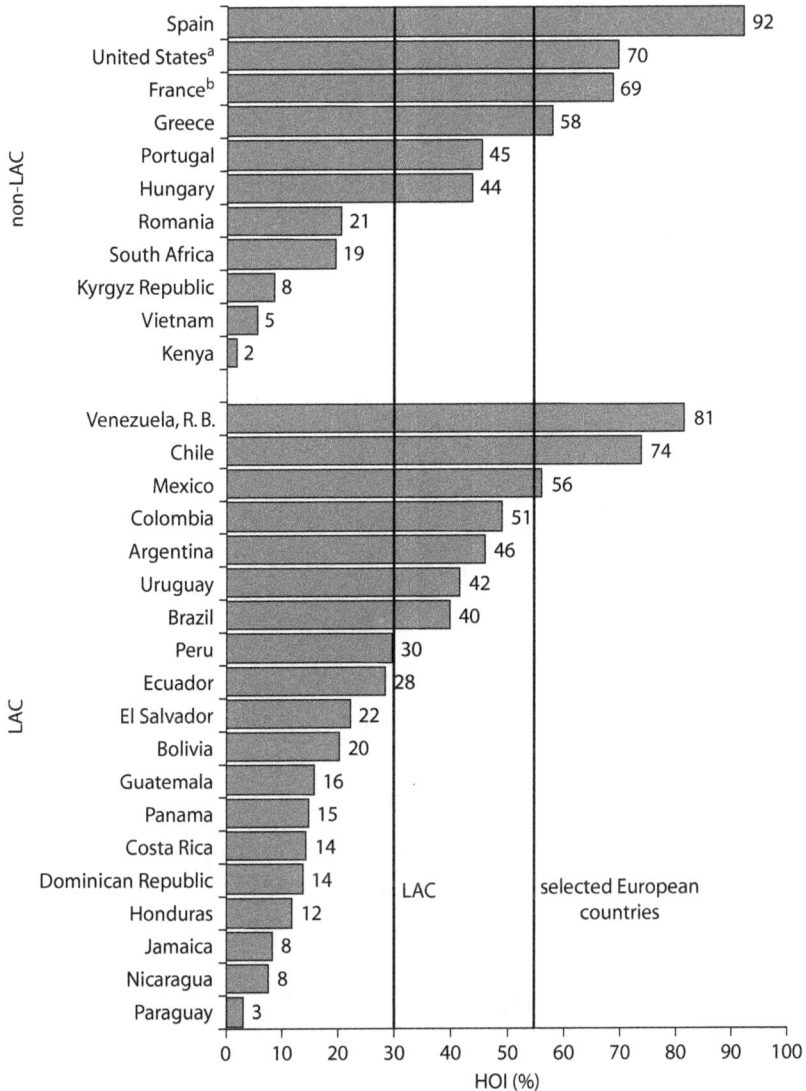

Source: Author's calculations using SEDLAC (Socio-Economic Database for Latin America and the Caribbean) data for LAC countries and IPUMS (Integrated Public Use Microdata Series) data for non-LAC countries.
a. For the United States, the most recent year is 1990.
b. For France, the most recent year is 1982.

Figure 3.2   HOI Access to Sanitation, Public and Private Connections

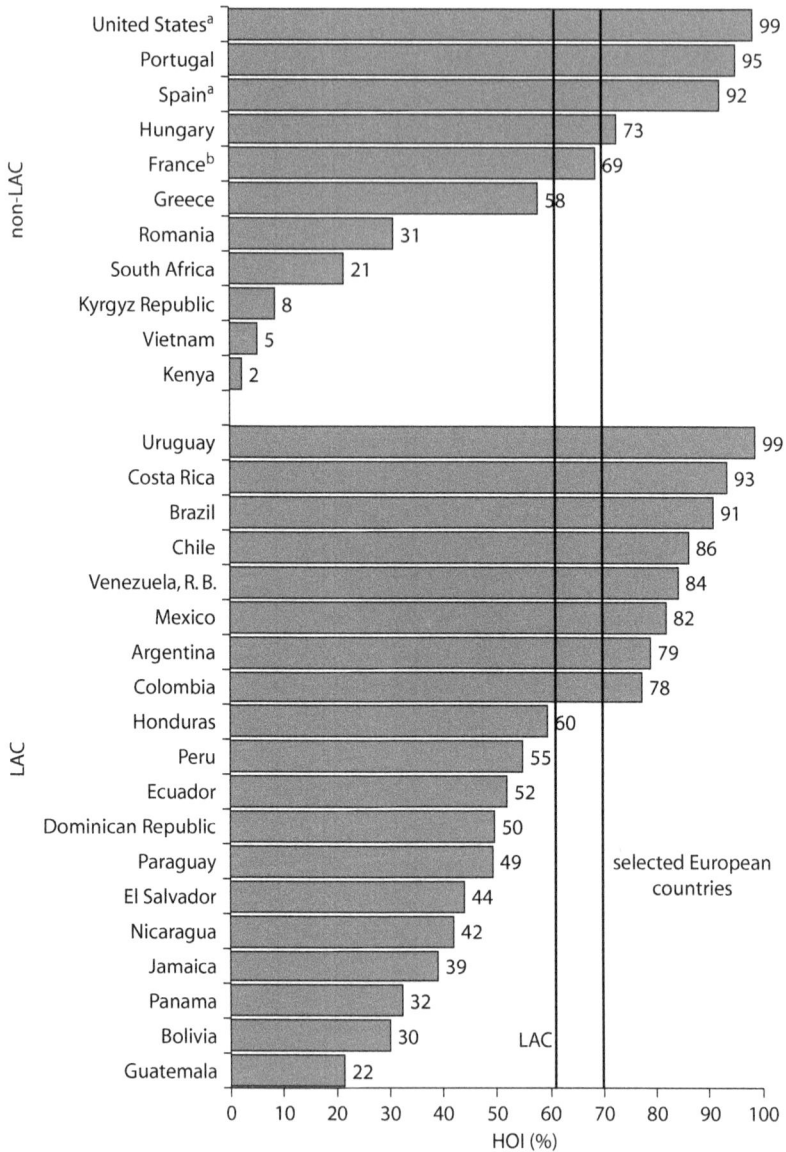

Source: Author's calculations using SEDLAC (Socio-Economic Database for Latin America and the Caribbean) data for LAC countries and IPUMS (Integrated Public Use Microdata Series) data for non-LAC countries.
a. For Spain and the United States, the most recent year is 1990.
b. For France, the most recent year is 1982.

to inequality of opportunity levels approximately twice as high in LAC than in European and North American countries when considering septic systems (tables A3.4a–b).

HOI for Freedom from Severe Overcrowding

The mean value of the freedom from severe overcrowding HOI in European countries is 67. Only three LAC countries are above this value: Brazil (88), Chile (84), and Costa Rica (78). The remaining countries are 10 or more percentage points below the mean (figure 3.3). In Spain—the highest scorer in this HOI—92 percent of the opportunities for access to overcrowded homes needed for universality are available and equitably distributed, compared with only 31 percent in Peru. Much of the freedom from severe overcrowding HOI gap is attributed to inequality of opportunity levels more than twice as high in LAC than European and North American countries (tables A3.5a–b).[6]

Understanding the Long-Run Evolution of the HOI

The IPUMS-International database contains information on multiple rounds of census data for several countries. The two longest time series available and analyzable were from the United States and France. This section exploits that time series by exploring the long-run evolution of the housing and sanitation HOI in these two countries. For the United States, data are available from each decennial census from 1960 to 2000; for 2005, data from the American Community Survey are used. In the case of France, the data are less consistently available although they span an equally long time period.

The Long-Run Evolution of the HOI for Severe Overcrowding

Over the past 45 years, the United States' HOI for freedom from severe overcrowding has improved by roughly 15 points (figure 3.4). The HOI improved rapidly in the first part of the period analyzed, and then growth slowed as the HOI approached universality. This might be in line with a notion that the last unit of a good or service is more costly to provide than the first.[7] The freedom from overcrowding HOI in France began from a much lower base than in the United States but improved much more quickly over a shorter period of time—from about 55 in 1968 to about 87 in 1999. Similar to the United States, improvements slowed as the HOI reached higher levels.

Figure 3.3   HOI Freedom from Severe Overcrowding, More than 1.5 People per Room

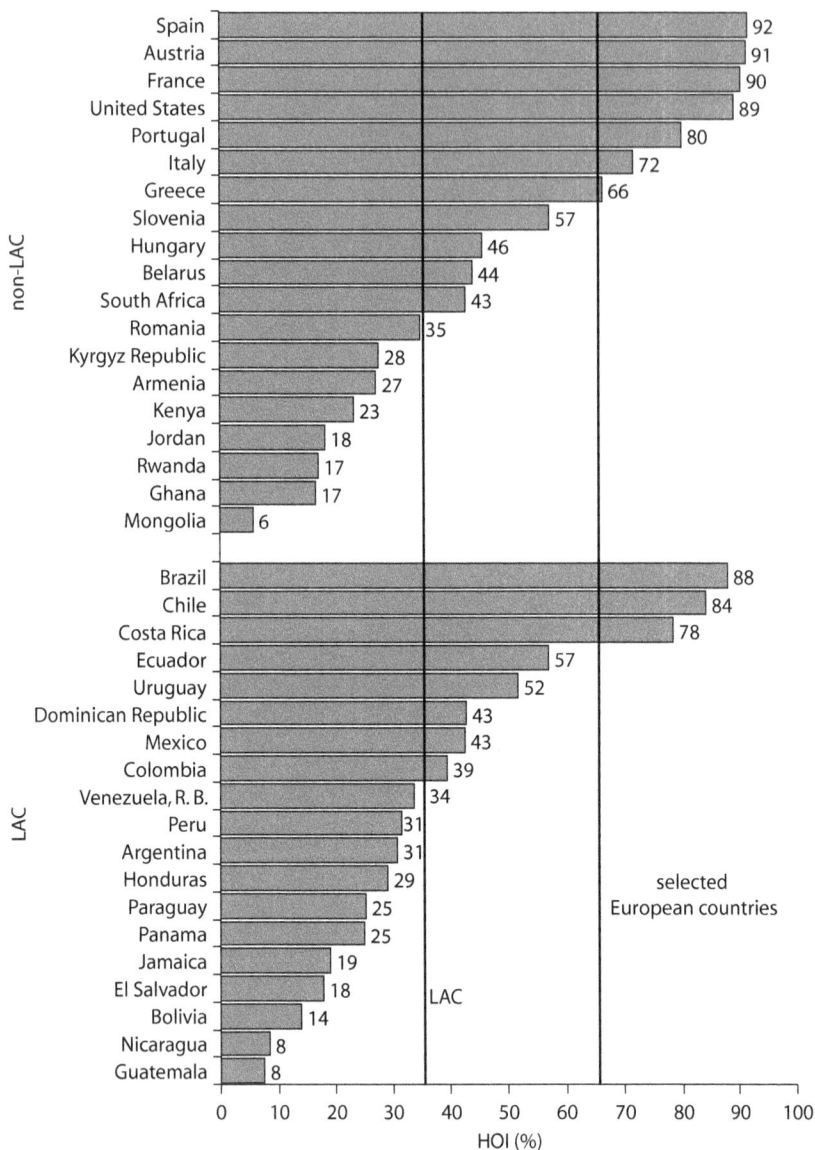

Source: Author's calculations using SEDLAC (Socio-Economic Database for Latin America and the Caribbean) data for LAC countries and IPUMS (Integrated Public Use Microdata Series) data for non-LAC countries.

Figure 3.4   HOI Overcrowding and Sanitation: United States 1960–2005 and France 1968–1999

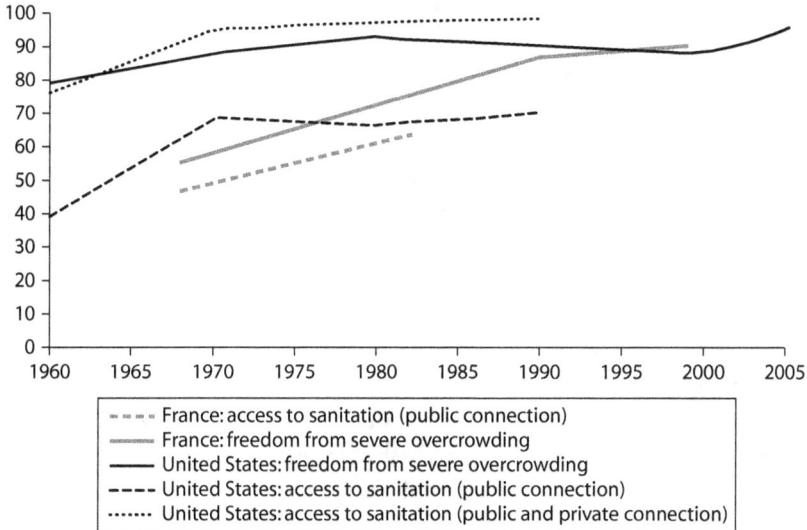

Legend:
- – – – France: access to sanitation (public connection)
- ———— France: freedom from severe overcrowding
- ———— United States: freedom from severe overcrowding
- – – – – United States: access to sanitation (public connection)
- ········ United States: access to sanitation (public and private connection)

Source: Authors' calculations using IPUMS data.
Note: We report all available data in this figure. Data are not available to compute access to septic tanks for France (see annex for details).

The Long-Run Evolution of the HOI for Adequate Sanitation

The HOI of access to adequate sanitation (public system only) shows much more similar values in United States and France than the overcrowding index, although improvement in the United States stagnates after 1970 whereas France shows steady growth. However, the French time series for this HOI is much shorter, making direct comparisons difficult. Including septic systems into the calculation brings the U.S. HOI up to near universality after 1970, but no data are available in France on septic systems to make a comparison. As with overcrowding, both countries showed faster growth rates when the HOI was low, with progress slowing as the HOI increased. For instance, for the United States, in 1960 the HOI for sanitation (public system + septic tanks) grew roughly 2 points per year between 1960 and 1970, but then only 0.3 points per year in 1970–80 and 0.1 points in 1980–90.

Conclusion

The analysis in this chapter illustrates that LAC countries still need to make significant progress to achieve the levels of equal opportunity most

OECD countries have achieved in the provision of basic services. This is particularly true regarding the quality of education, where LAC countries all score below even the lowest-achieving countries in Europe and North America. Housing HOIs are also below European averages, but in this case some LAC countries have reached and even exceeded the median European HOI scores.

Despite gains in educational outcomes, the gap between the education HOI in LAC and Europe and North America remains large. All LAC countries included in this study have a lower HOI than any of the countries analyzed in Europe and North America on opportunities for accessing quality education. The countries with the highest HOIs for reading, mathematics, and science in LAC are considerably behind the countries with the lowest performance in Europe and North America. Much of the overall education HOI gap is attributed to inequality-of-opportunity levels often two or three times higher in LAC than European and North American countries. Wealth status is the circumstance most strongly associated with inequality of opportunity in reading, mathematics, and science in LAC countries.

The results on housing cover two areas relevant for policy makers: access to sanitation and freedom from severe overcrowding. Only two of 18 LAC countries analyzed were above the average for European countries in access to sanitation via a public connection, and only seven were above the European average when the definition included septic tanks. The average value of the freedom from overcrowding HOI was 67 among European countries. Only three LAC countries—Chile, Costa Rica, and Brazil—are above this value, with the remaining countries five or more points below.

Analyzing the expansion of the HOI for housing opportunities in the United States and France from the 1960s indicates that HOI levels are initially low, experience fast growth rates, and then slow as the HOI reaches a high level. This suggests that LAC countries may follow a similar pattern—achieving strong gains in the equitable provision of basic services earlier in the development process, and then slowing as countries come close to universal provision. The evidence from chapter 2 on trends in LAC over time coincides with this finding in certain respects.

This chapter underscores that the current generation of children in Latin America have fewer opportunities of accessing key goods and services than their counterparts in Europe and North America, and that existing opportunities are distributed less equitably. The literature suggests that it will be more difficult for these children, endowed with these more limited opportunities, to enjoy psychological and physical good health as children and to be motivated and equipped to pursue their interests and reach their potential as adults. This suggests that important barriers remain in all regions analyzed, but particularly in Latin America, to ensure that the next generation of children faces a level playing field in obtaining opportunities needed to develop themselves.

Annex

Table A3.1   Circumstance Variables Used in PISA Analysis

Variable	Definition
Child's gender	Dummy variable taking on a value of 1 for male
School location	Dummy variables taking on a value of 1 for each of the following categories: • A village, hamlet, or rural area (fewer than 3,000 people) • A small town (3,000 to about 15,000 people) • A town (15,000 to about 100,000 people) • A city (100,000 to about 1,000,000 people) The dummy for a large city (with over 1,000,000 people) was excluded to avoid collinearity.
Father's education	Dummy variables taking on a value of 1 for each of the following categories: • Completed ISCED 3A (upper secondary, general) • Completed ISCED 3B, 3C (upper secondary, vocational) • Completed ISCED 2 (lower secondary) • Completed ISCED 1 (primary) • Did not complete ISCED 1 (did not complete primary) The dummy for tertiary education was excluded to avoid collinearity.
Mother's education	Dummy variables taking on a value of 1 for each of the following categories: • Completed ISCED 3A (upper secondary, general) • Completed ISCED 3B, 3C (upper secondary, vocational) • Completed ISCED 2 (lower secondary) • Completed ISCED 1 (primary) • Did not complete ISCED 1 (did not complete primary) The dummy for tertiary education was excluded to avoid collinearity.
Wealth index	The wealth index is the score of the first principal component created using 14 common household assets available in the data for all countries.
Father's occupation	Dummy variables taking on a value of 1 for each of the eight categories of ISCO occupation classification on four digit basis. The dummy for primary occupations was excluded to avoid collinearity.

Source: Authors.

Table A3.2 Profile of Inequality of Proficiency at Level 2 in Reading: Relative Importance of the Six Circumstances by Country

Country	Most important	2	3	4	5	6
Argentina	Socioeconomic status	Gender	Father's occupation	School location	Mother's education	Father's education
Brazil	Socioeconomic status	Gender	Father's occupation	Father's education	Mother's education	School location
Canada	Socioeconomic status	Gender	Father's occupation	Father's education	Mother's education	—
Chile	Socioeconomic status	Gender	School location	Mother's education	Father's occupation	Father's education
Colombia	Socioeconomic status	School location	Father's occupation	Mother's education	Father's education	Gender
England	Father's occupation	Socioeconomic status	Gender	Father's education	School location	Mother's education
France	Socioeconomic status	Father's occupation	Gender	Mother's education	Father's education	—
Germany	Socioeconomic status	Gender	Father's occupation	Mother's education	Father's education	School location
Italy	Gender	Socioeconomic status	School location	Father's occupation	Father's education	Mother's education
Mexico	School location	Gender	Socioeconomic status	Mother's education	Father's occupation	Father's education
Norway	Gender	Socioeconomic status	Father's occupation	Mother's education	Father's education	School location
Portugal	Socioeconomic status	Father's occupation	Gender	Mother's education	Father's education	School location
Spain	Socioeconomic status	Father's occupation	Gender	Mother's education	Father's education	School location
Sweden	Gender	Socioeconomic status	Father's occupation	Father's education	Mother's education	School location
Uruguay	Gender	Socioeconomic status	Mother's education	Father's occupation	School location	Father's education

Source: Authors' calculations based on PISA data.
Note: — = data not available.

Table A3.3a IPUMS Samples Analyzed

	Country	Year	Census (%)	Households	Persons	Sanitation (public)	Sanitation (public + septic)	Overcrowding
	Europe							
1	Austria	2001	10	341,035	803,471	N	N	Y
2	Armenia	2001	10	81,929	326,560	N	N	Y
3	Belarus	1999	10	385,508	990,706	N	N	Y
4	France	1999	5	1,219,323	2,934,758	N	N	Y
5	Greece	2001	10	367,438	1,028,884	Y	Y	Y
6	Hungary	2001	5	227,252	510,502	Y	N	Y
7	Italy	2001	5	1,168,044	2,990,739	N	N	Y
8	Portugal	2001	5	258,843	517,026	Y	Y	Y
9	Romania	2002	10	732,016	2,137,967	Y	Y	Y
10	Slovenia	2002	10	63,637	179,632	N	N	Y
11	Spain	2001	5	714,473	2,039,274	N	Y	Y
	North America							
12	United States	2000	5	6,184,438	14,081,466	N	N	Y
	East and Central Asia							
13	Kyrgyz Republic	1999	10	110,285	476,886	Y	Y	Y
14	Mongolia	2000	10	55,795	243,725	N	N	Y
15	Vietnam	1999	3	534,139	2,368,167	N	N	N
	Middle East and Africa							
16	Ghana	2000	10	397,097	1,894,133	N	N	Y
17	Jordan	2004	10	97,343	510,646	N	N	Y
18	Kenya	1999	5	317,106	1,407,547	Y	Y	Y
19	Rwanda	2002	10	191,719	843,392	Y	Y	Y
20	South Africa	2001	10	991,543	3,725,655	Y	Y	Y
21	Uganda	2002	10	529,271	2,497,449	N	N	N

Source: Authors, based on IPUMS data.

Note: Additional countries will be included for Asia. Canada could not be analyzed because persons are not organized into households. This means we do not have information on parental characteristics. Y = yes; N = no.

Table A3.3b   Access to Sanitation in Selected LAC Countries (Public System)

	Coverage	D-index	Penalty	HOI	Standard error
Argentina	53	13	7	46	0.5
Bolivia	32	36	11	20	0.4
Brazil	47	16	7	40	0.2
Chile	82	11	9	74	0.1
Colombia	64	23	15	49	0.3
Costa Rica	22	35	8	14	0.3
Dominican Republic	19	28	5	14	0.4
Ecuador	41	31	13	28	0.3
El Salvador	36	38	14	22	0.3
Guatemala	29	46	13	16	0.2
Honduras	24	51	12	12	0.1
Jamaica	15	43	6	8	0.3
Mexico	68	17	12	56	0.3
Nicaragua	15	50	8	8	0.2
Panama	25	42	10	15	0.3
Paraguay	5	44	2	3	0.2
Peru	46	36	16	30	0.2
Uruguay	49	14	7	42	0.4
Venezuela, R. B.	86	5	5	81	0.2

Source: Authors' calculations using SEDLAC data.

Table A3.3c   Access to Sanitation in Selected Non-LAC Countries (Public System)

	Coverage	D-index	Penalty	HOI	Standard error
France[a]	70	3	2	69	0.06
Greece[a]	64	9	6	58	0.13
Hungary[a]	50	12	6	44	0.16
Kenya	5	65	3	2	0.01
Kyrgyz Republic	17	51	9	8	0.05
Portugal	59	22	13	45	0.16
Romania	39	48	19	21	0.04
South Africa	36	47	17	19	0.02
Spain[a]	93	1	1	92	0.05
United States[a]	73	4	3	70	0.03
Vietnam	13	58	8	5	0.03

Source: Authors' calculations using IPUMS data.
a. Denotes that data on all circumstances were not available for this country. The specification used to compute the HOI thus differs slightly compared with the rest of the countries in this table.

Table A3.4a   Access to Sanitation in Selected LAC Countries (Public System and Septic Tank)

	Coverage	D-index	Penalty	HOI	Standard error
Argentina	83	5	4	79	0.5
Bolivia	44	32	14	30	0.6
Brazil	93	3	2	91	0.1
Chile	91	5	5	86	0.1
Colombia	84	8	7	77	0.4
Costa Rica	95	2	2	93	0.2
Dominican Republic	61	19	12	50	0.6
Ecuador	64	19	12	52	0.4
El Salvador	54	19	10	44	0.4
Guatemala	35	39	14	22	0.3
Honduras	67	10	7	60	0.3
Jamaica	49	20	10	39	0.6
Mexico	88	7	6	82	0.3
Nicaragua	50	16	8	42	0.5
Panama	46	29	13	32	0.5
Paraguay	62	21	13	49	0.6
Peru	65	16	10	55	0.3
Uruguay	99	0	0	99	0.1
Venezuela, R. B.	88	5	4	84	0.2

Source: Authors' calculations using SEDLAC data.

Table A3.4b   Access to Sanitation in Selected Non-LAC Countries (Public System and Septic Tank)

	Coverage	D-index	Penalty	HOI	Standard error
France[a]	70	3	2	69	0.06
Greece[a]	64	9	6	58	0.13
Hungary[a]	77	6	4	73	0.16
Kenya	6	64	4	2	0.01
Kyrgyz Republic	17	51	9	8	0.05
Portugal	97	1	1	95	0.08
Romania	48	36	17	31	0.06
South Africa	38	44	17	21	0.03
Spain[a]	93	1	1	92	0.05
United States[a]	99	0	0	99	0.01
Vietnam	13	58	8	5	0.03

Source: Authors' calculations using IPUMS data.
a. Denotes that data on all circumstances were not available for this country. The specification used to compute the HOI thus differs slightly compared with the rest of the countries in this table.

Table A3.5a   Freedom from Severe Overcrowding, LAC Countries

	Coverage	D-index	Penalty	HOI	Standard error
Argentina	44	30	13	31	0.4
Bolivia	20	31	6	14	0.5
Brazil	92	5	4	88	0.1
Chile	88	4	4	84	0.2
Colombia	52	24	12	39	0.4
Costa Rica	85	8	7	78	0.4
Dominican Republic	55	23	13	43	0.5
Ecuador	67	15	10	57	0.4
El Salvador	28	37	11	18	0.3
Guatemala	15	49	7	8	0.2
Honduras	41	29	12	29	0.2
Jamaica	28	33	9	19	0.4
Mexico	63	18	11	51	0.3
Nicaragua	16	46	7	8	0.2
Panama	38	34	13	25	0.4
Paraguay	37	31	12	25	0.5
Peru	41	23	9	31	0.3
Uruguay	64	19	12	52	0.3
Venezuela, R. B.	46	27	12	34	0.2

Source: Authors' calculations using SEDLAC data.

Table A3.5b   Freedom from Severe Overcrowding, Non-LAC Countries

	Coverage	D-index	Penalty	HOI	Standard error
Armenia	33	17	6	27	0.15
Austria[a]	94	2	2	91	0.08
Belarus	50	13	6	44	0.11
France[a]	93	3	3	90	0.04
Ghana	21	21	4	17	0.04
Greece[a]	74	10	7	66	0.11
Hungary[a]	56	18	10	46	0.15
Italy[a]	78	9	7	72	0.07
Jordan	28	35	10	18	0.07
Kenya	30	22	6	23	0.05
Kyrgyz Republic	35	21	8	28	0.10
Mongolia[a]	10	41	4	6	0.09
Portugal	86	7	6	80	0.14
Romania	45	23	10	35	0.07
Rwanda	26	33	9	17	0.05
Slovenia	63	9	6	57	0.33
South Africa	52	17	9	43	0.04
Spain[a]	94	3	2	92	0.05
United States[a]	92	4	3	89	0.02

Source: Authors' calculations using IPUMS data.
a. Denotes that data on all circumstances were not available for this country. The specification used to compute the HOI thus differs slightly compared with the rest of the countries in this table.

Table A3.6a   Freedom from Overcrowding, LAC Countries

	Coverage	D-index	Penalty	HOI	Standard error
Argentina	20	44	9	11	0.2
Bolivia	8	48	4	4	0.2
Brazil	79	12	10	69	0.1
Chile	71	13	9	62	0.3
Colombia	26	40	11	16	0.3
Costa Rica	63	19	12	51	0.4
Dominican Republic	28	38	11	17	0.4
Ecuador	44	30	13	31	0.3
El Salvador	13	50	6	6	0.2
Guatemala	6	62	4	2	0.1
Honduras	23	45	10	13	0.1
Jamaica	12	51	6	6	0.2
Mexico	41	31	13	29	0.3
Nicaragua	5	59	3	2	0.1
Panama	18	48	9	9	0.3
Paraguay	17	42	7	10	0.3
Peru	19	36	7	12	0.2
Uruguay	37	34	12	24	0.2
Venezuela, R. B.	22	42	9	13	0.1

Source: Authors' calculations using SEDLAC data.

Table A3.6b   Freedom from Overcrowding, Non-LAC Countries

	Coverage	D-index	Penalty	HOI	Standard error
Armenia	9	37	3	6	0.07
Austria[a]	80	8	6	73	0.12
Belarus	17	29	5	12	0.07
France[a]	73	12	9	64	0.06
Ghana	9	34	3	6	0.02
Greece[a]	39	22	9	31	0.10
Hungary[a]	27	28	8	19	0.12
Italy[a]	43	23	10	33	0.07
Jordan	9	57	5	4	0.03
Kenya	13	34	4	9	0.03
Kyrgyz Republic	12	40	5	7	0.05
Mongolia[a]	3	52	1	1	0.04
Portugal	60	16	10	50	0.15
Romania	18	33	6	12	0.04
Rwanda	10	53	5	4	0.02
Slovenia	30	17	5	25	0.28
South Africa	30	30	9	21	0.03
Spain[a]	82	7	6	76	0.07
United States[a]	82	8	7	75	0.03

Source: Authors' calculations using IPUMS data.
a. Denotes that data on all circumstances were not available for this country. The specification used to compute the HOI thus differs slightly compared with the rest of the countries in this table.

Notes

1. The groups are below level 1, levels 1 to 5 for reading, and levels 1 to 6 for science and mathematics.

2. Data for reading in the United States PISA 2006 are not available because of an error in the printed test booklet that distorted the results.

3. It is important to remember that the specific D-indices do not add up to the overall D-index; that is, this exercise does not have additive properties.

4. We explored the possibility of including an asset index. However, consistent information on asset ownership was not available for all countries.

5. Table A3.4b reports the results from the most recent round of household surveys analyzed in chapter 2. Table A3.4b complements these results using data from censuses available in the IPUMS database.

6. In some countries the surveys do not allow us to distinguish either kitchens or bathrooms from the total number of rooms in the household: Brazil, 2008; Costa Rica, 2009; and República Bolivariana de Venezuela, 2005. Thus, in these cases, the number of rooms is greater than in the rest of the countries. In the case of Honduras, we were able to remove only bathrooms from the count of number of rooms. The estimates for all countries where kitchens or bathrooms are included are therefore higher than they would be if we were able to remove the kitchen from the count of the number of rooms.

7. This slowing of the HOI growth rate at approach to universality would imply in most cases that the actual arrival time to universality would be slower than what a linear growth assumption would suggest. In light of this finding, the arrival time to universality in LAC discussed in chapter 2 should be considered as "optimistic" projections of the LAC expected trend.

Bibliography

Chombart de Lauwe. 1956. *P. H. Chombart de Lauwe: La Vie quotidienne des familles ouvrières*. Paris: CNRS.

Coggan, D., D. J. P. Barker, H. Inskip, and G. Wield. 1993. "Housing in Early Life and Later Mortality." *Journal of Epidemiology and Community Health* 47: 345–48.

Corak, Miles, Lori Curtis, and Shelley Phipps. 2010. "Economic Mobility, Family Background, and the Well-being of Children in the United States and Canada." IZA Discussion Paper No. 4814, IZA, Bonn, Germany.

Currie, Janet, and Aaron Yelowitz. 2000. "Are Public Housing Projects Good for Kids?" *Journal of Public Economics* 75: 99–124.

Fuller, T. D., J. N. Edwards, S. Sermsri, and S. Vorakitphokatorn. 1993. "Housing, Stress, and Physical Well-being: Evidence from Thailand." *Social Science Medicine* 36(11): 1417–28.

Goux, Dominique, and Eric Maurin. 2005. "The Effect of Overcrowded Housing on Children's Performance at School." *Journal of Public Economics* 89: 797–819.

Gove, W. A., M. Hughes, and O. R. Galle. 1979. "Overcrowding in the Home: An Empirical Investigation of Its Possible Pathological Consequences." *American Sociological Review* 44: 55–80.

HUD (U.S. Department of Housing and Urban Development). 2007. "Measuring Overcrowding in Housing." HUD, Washington, DC.

Marshy, Mona. 1999. "Social and Psychological Effects of Overcrowding in Palestinian Refugee Camps in the West Bank and Gaza—Literature Review and Preliminary Assessment of the Problem." International Development Research Centre, Ottawa. http://www.idrc.ca/uploads/user-S/11244731091 marshy.htm.

OECD (Organisation for Economic Co-operation and Development). 2007. "PISA 2006: Science Competencies for Tomorrow's World Executive Summary." OECD, Paris. Data available at http://www.oecd.org/dataoecd/0/47/42025182.pdf.

Office of the Deputy Prime Minister, London. 2004. "The Impact of Overcrowding on Health and Education: A Review of Evidence and Literature." Office of the Deputy Prime Minister, London.

UNICEF (United Nations Children's Fund). 2006. "Children and Water, Sanitation and Hygiene: The Evidence." Human Development Report Office Occasional Paper, United Nations Development Fund, New York.

CHAPTER 4

Human Opportunities at the Subnational Level in Latin America and the Caribbean

Spatial inequalities—both in terms of outcomes, such as income and poverty, and in access to critical opportunities—have received considerable attention in the literature. Not only do spatial inequalities remain marked, but they have the potential to create significant political tensions, and they present an actionable policy challenge.

This chapter explores inequalities in the Human Opportunity Index (HOI) at the subnational level (region, province, department, or state) in Latin America and the Caribbean (LAC). The chapter also analyzes whether the dispersion of subnational (SN) HOIs grows or decreases with the level of the HOI and the structure of government (degree of decentralization) and outlines possible fiscal instruments that can be used to accelerate equality of opportunities across subnational regions.

Not surprisingly, the chapter discovers significant heterogeneity in subnational opportunities across time, countries, and the specific opportunity dimensions analyzed. It presents stylized facts on overall equality of opportunities at the subnational level as well as on access to housing and education opportunities. The analysis shows convergence between states with high and low initial HOI levels, albeit at a rather slow pace. This convergence appears more in educational opportunities compared with opportunities to access quality housing.

This chapter is organized as follows. Section 4.1 describes the main findings regarding subregional HOIs across countries. It considers stylized facts for housing and education opportunities across the top- and bottom-ranked subnational regions. Section 4.2 analyzes different measures of dispersion of SN HOIs and how dispersion may relate to different national and regional policies, most notably the degree of political and fiscal decentralization. Section 4.3 discusses possible ways to equalize opportunities across regions, supporting the *World Development Report 2009* (World Bank 2009b) message that opportunities should be equalized by leveling the playing field, rather than by seeking uniformity in outcomes. Section 4.4 offers concluding remarks.

The Subnational Human Opportunity Indices: Some Stylized Facts

A series of subnational Human Opportunity Indices (SN HOIs) is estimated using data from 30 household surveys for 15 LAC countries over a period of more than a decade (1995–2009). The analysis employs the same basic services, circumstances, and overall methodology as the national indices in chapter 2. Together the surveys represent roughly 165 subnational governments from 15 LAC countries (tables A4.1 and A4.2).[1]

The analysis finds significant heterogeneity in children's access to basic services across subregions or subnational governments in the countries considered, with a much wider range than between overall national-level HOIs.[2] The spread extends from a high of 97 for Tierra del Fuego in Argentina to lows of 29 in the Atlantic Region, Nicaragua, and the indigenous Comarcas, Panama.

The ranking of subnational regions is roughly similar to the national ranking by HOI. Chile and Uruguay are the top countries in terms of the national HOI. Of the 165 provinces considered, the first 50 provinces include 17 from Uruguay, 17 from Argentina, 11 from Chile, 3 from Colombia, 1 from Peru, and 1 from Costa Rica. All except two of Uruguay's provinces (95 percent) are among the top 50; Chile has 85 percent (all except two); and Argentina 70 percent, whereas Colombia has only 30 percent (three out of nine provinces).[3]

Similarly, the lowest-ranked SN HOIs tend to come from the countries with the lowest national HOI scores. All the regions of El Salvador, Guatemala, and Nicaragua are included in the 50 lowest-ranked SN HOIs, except for their capital cities (table A4.2). Uniquely, Peru has regions in both the top 50 and bottom 50 provinces: one in the top and three in the bottom. More than 60 percent of the subregions of Brazil, Ecuador, Honduras, and Panama are in the middle ranking, and the rest in the bottom. They seem to be in the "lower-middle class" in terms of provincial distribution among this group of countries. On the other hand, Colombia and Costa Rica also have more than 60 percent of their SN HOIs in the middle with the rest in the top, and hence are more "upper-middle class." Brazil and Colombia, two of the most unequal countries in the region in terms of income inequality and regional income disparities, do not appear so unequal in terms of the spatial distribution of opportunities.[4]

Opportunities to access basic goods and services are systematically higher in the capital cities. Comparing the overall HOI by capital city and the rest of the country, Bogotá, Santiago, Buenos Aires, and Montevideo are the top ranked, and all capital cities provide more opportunities than other areas of their countries (figure 4.1).[5]

Among the lower-ranked countries, the gap is greater between the capital cities and the rest of the nation (figure 4.2). Not only are the HOIs of the capital cities higher than the rest of their respective countries, but also the higher the HOI, the lower the gap in opportunities between capital and the rest of the country.

Disaggregating SN HOIs by education and housing opportunities shows that access to opportunities is more uneven for housing than for education (figures 4.3 and 4.4). It also reveals that the gap between capital cities and the rest of the country is greater for housing than for education. The relative ranking of capital cities does not perfectly match the overall national HOI ranking. The capitals of Brazil and Costa Rica have the highest rankings for housing, whereas the capitals of Colombia and Peru have the highest ranking for education, despite the fact that these are not the top countries in the national HOIs.[6]

The dispersion of SN HOI scores for education and housing does not necessarily follow similar patterns. Although Peru has relatively higher HOIs for education across subnational regions (the areas outside of Lima score in the top third of the HOI for education), it has low HOIs for housing outside of Lima (figures 4.3 and 4.4). In Brazil, HOIs are lower in education, but the gap between the capital city and the rest of the country is greater for housing: The HOI for education in the capital is 65, and in the rest of the country it is 64, whereas the housing HOI is 99 for Brasilia and 82 for the rest of Brazil.

There is evidence of a decreasing gap over time between capital cities and other areas of the country for access to basic services, as well as an overall convergence in levels among the subnational regions. Comparing

Figure 4.1 Overall HOI circa 2008 for the Capital City and the Rest of the Country

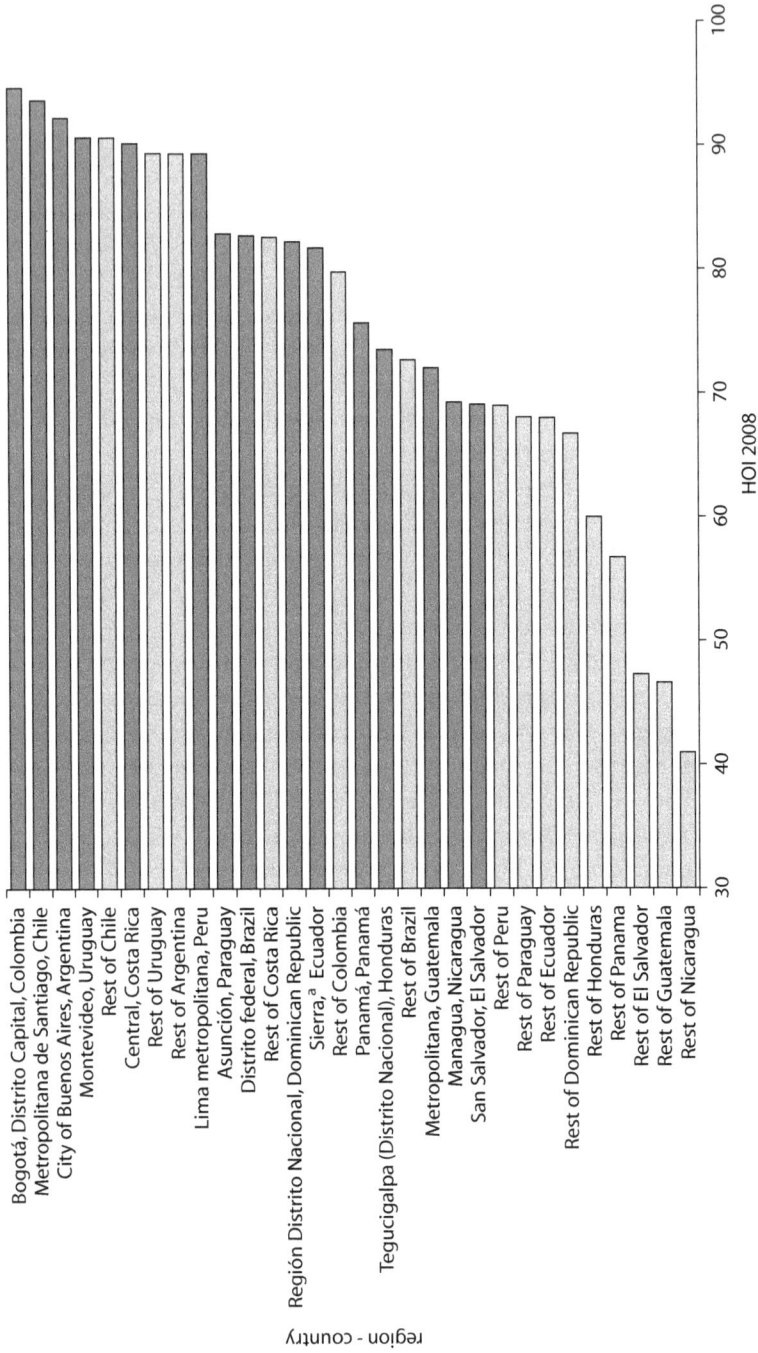

region - country

HOI 2008

Bogotá, Distrito Capital, Colombia
Metropolitana de Santiago, Chile
City of Buenos Aires, Argentina
Montevideo, Uruguay
Rest of Chile
Central, Costa Rica
Rest of Uruguay
Rest of Argentina
Lima metropolitana, Peru
Asunción, Paraguay
Distrito federal, Brazil
Rest of Costa Rica
Región Distrito Nacional, Dominican Republic
Sierra,[a] Ecuador
Rest of Colombia
Panamá, Panamá
Tegucigalpa (Distrito Nacional), Honduras
Rest of Brazil
Metropolitana, Guatemala
Managua, Nicaragua
San Salvador, El Salvador
Rest of Peru
Rest of Paraguay
Rest of Ecuador
Rest of Dominican Republic
Rest of Honduras
Rest of Panama
Rest of El Salvador
Rest of Guatemala
Rest of Nicaragua

Source: Authors' calculations using SEDLAC data.
a. Includes Quito, the capital city.

Figure 4.2   Overall HOI circa 2008 for the Capital City and the Rest of the Country

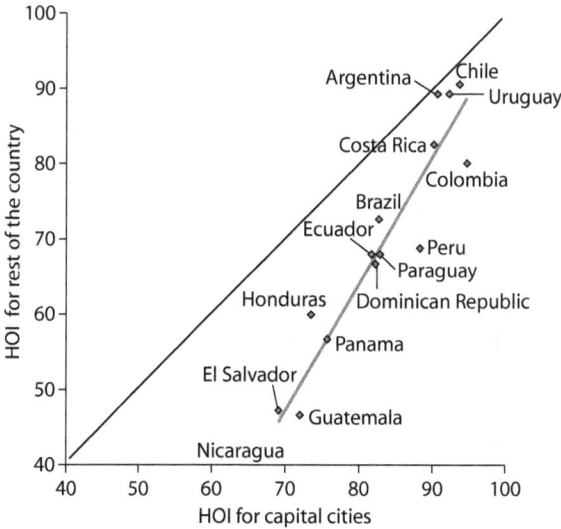

Source: Authors' calculations using SEDLAC data.
Note: The fact that capital city HOIs are below the 45 degree line indicates that they have higher HOI scores than the rest of the country.

annual overall HOI growth from the mid-1990s to 2008 between capital cities and the areas outside these cities suggests that, in general, the highest increases in the overall HOIs were attained outside the capital cities, and in particular in areas that had lower services in the mid-1990s (figure 4.5). In the approximately 13 years considered, 7 out of the 10 greatest improvements in the HOIs were experienced by the areas outside the capitals of Brazil, Ecuador, Guatemala, Nicaragua, Panama, Paraguay, and Peru. Among the 10 lowest growth areas, 8 are capital cities—Buenos Aires, Panamá (Panama City), Asunción, Montevideo, Bogotá, Santiago, San José, and San Salvador.[7] Plotting the overall HOI growth rate against the HOI in levels indicates convergence of opportunities across subnational regions (figure 4.6). The results reveal that the higher the HOI, the lower the rate of change.[8]

Further evidence for convergence can be found in graphing the HOI circa 1995 against the HOI circa 2008: The trend line is flatter than 45 percent, suggesting that the rate of change was smaller for regions with a higher HOI in 2008 (figure 4.7). The time convergence seems more pronounced in the case of education than in housing (figures 4.3 and 4.4).

Figure 4.3 HOI in Housing circa 2008 for the Capital City and the Rest of the Country

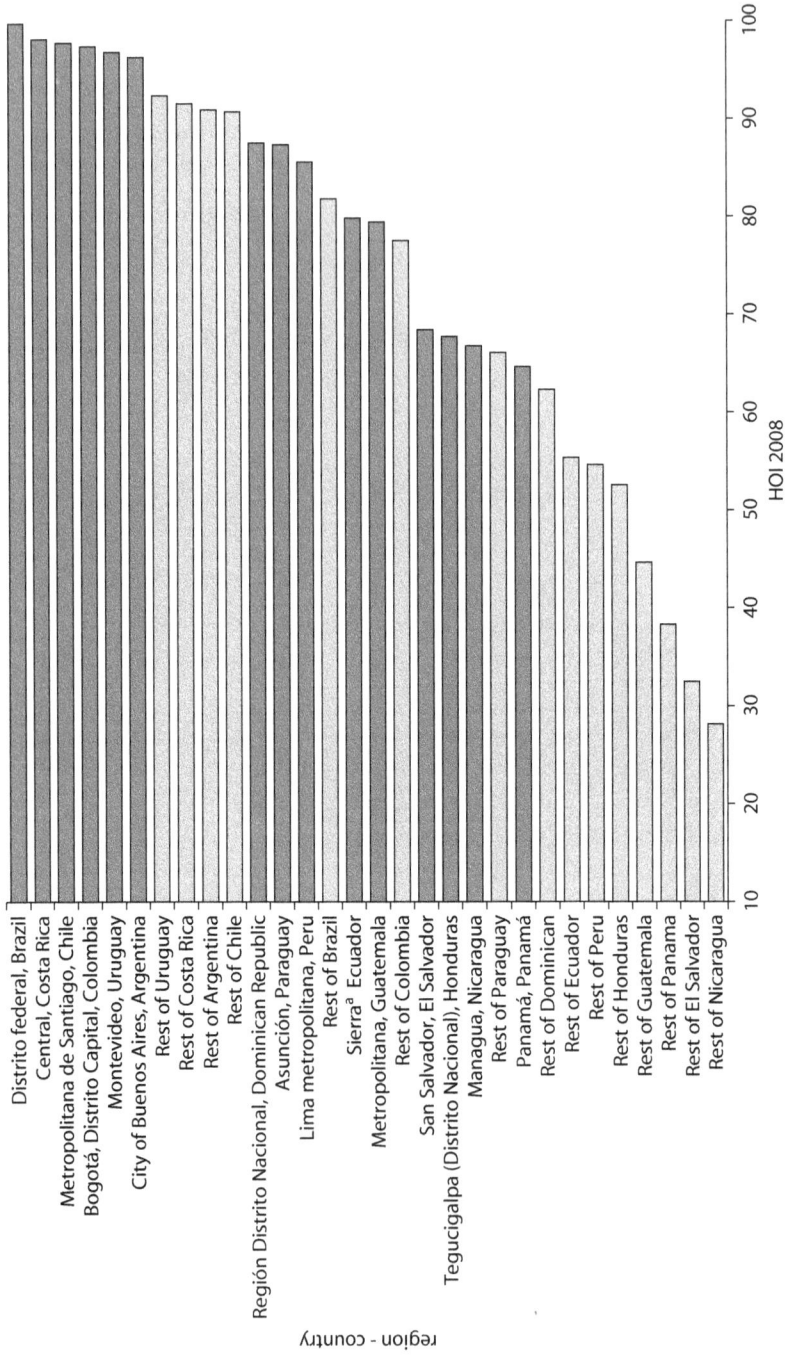

Source: Authors' calculations using SEDLAC data.

a. Includes Quito, the capital city.

Figure 4.4   HOI in Education circa 2008 for the Capital City and the Rest of the Country

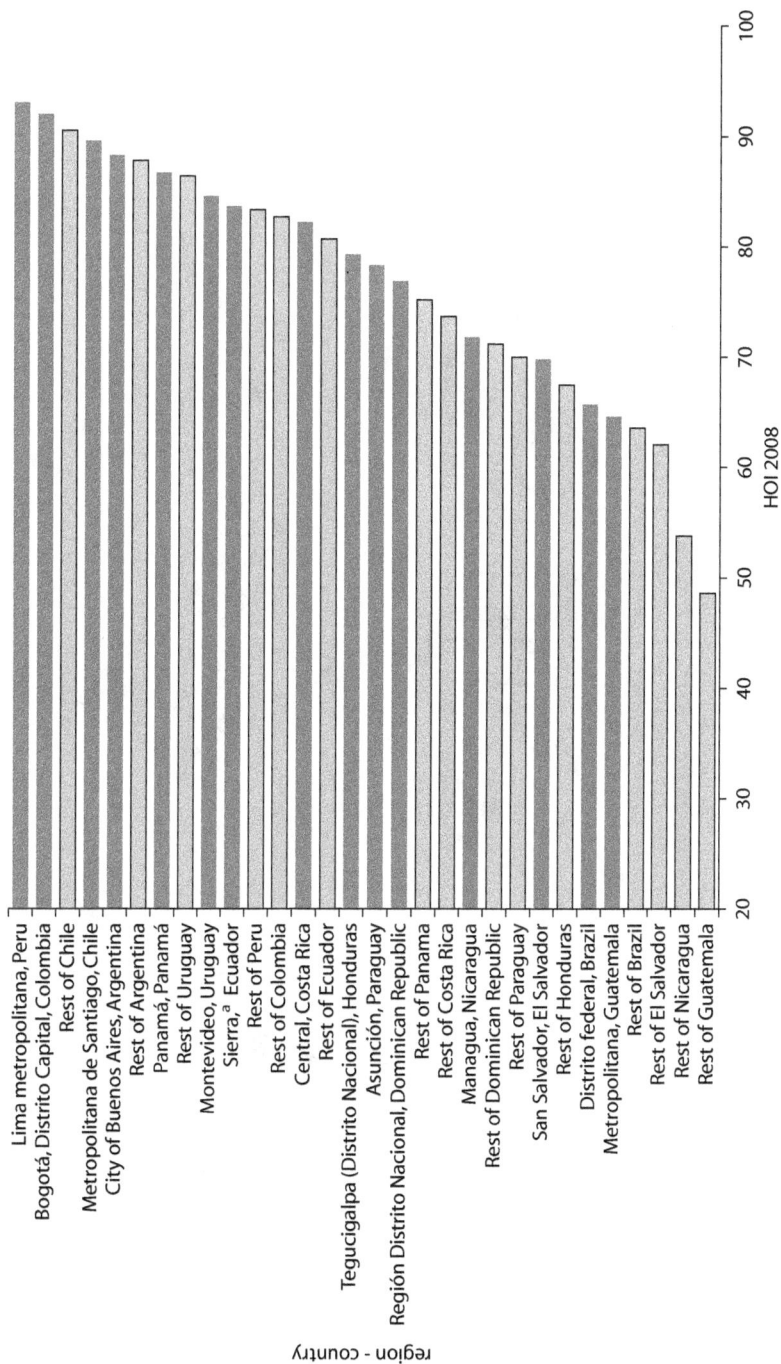

Source: Authors' calculations using SEDLAC data.
a. Includes Quito, the capital city.

Figure 4.5   Annual Growth of HOI between circa 1995 and 2008: Capital Cities versus the Rest of the Country

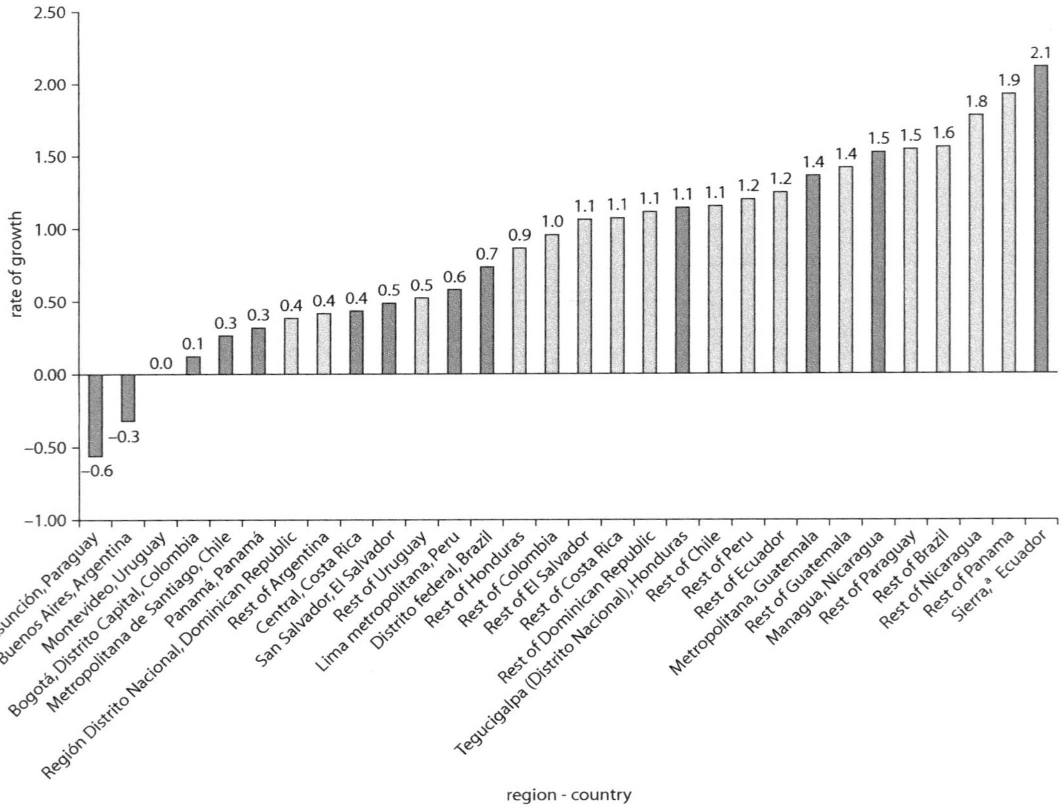

Source: Authors' calculations using SEDLAC data.
a. Includes Quito, the capital city.

Figure 4.6   Annual Growth of HOI between circa 1995 and 2008

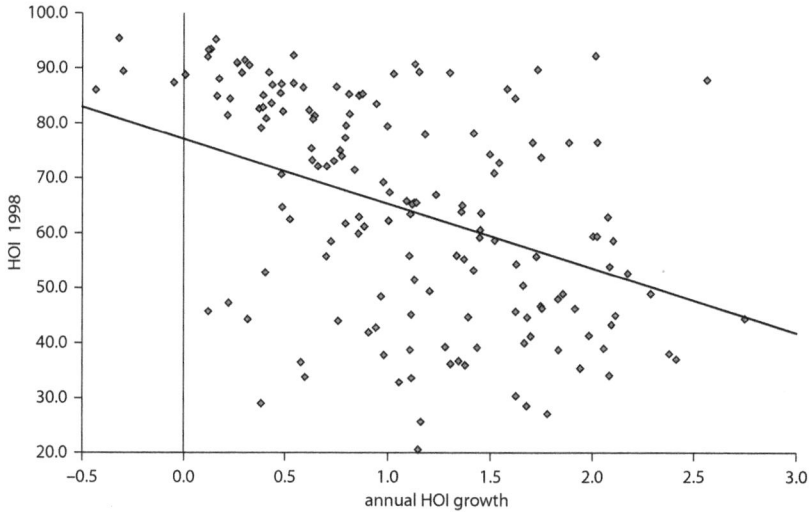

Source: Authors' calculations using SEDLAC data.

Heterogeneity in Subnational HOIs

In this section we discuss two issues: (1) the relationship between national and SN HOIs, and (2) whether more decentralized countries are more effective in equalizing SN HOIs.

Relationship between National and Subnational HOIs

Many economists interested in regional differences tend to examine variation in regional poverty outcomes, focusing mainly on income inequality (Shankar and Shah 2003; Von Braun and Grote 2002). Although it is valid to analyze income inequality across regions of a given country, there is less consensus on what type of "just" redistributive policy would follow from the analysis. Income (or geographic gross domestic product [GDP]) equality depends on factors outside the control of policy makers, and not only on equality of opportunity but also on personal responsibility and random shocks (luck).[9] Much more consensus exists on creating redistributive justice by equalizing opportunities—leveling the playing field—especially for children.

No single statistical measure can capture the myriad dimensions of regional disparities. The last section showed that, although disparities tend to be larger in regions with lower HOIs, these same regions tend to grow faster than those with higher HOIs. The standard deviation of overall,

Figure 4.7   Overall HOI circa 1995 and 2008

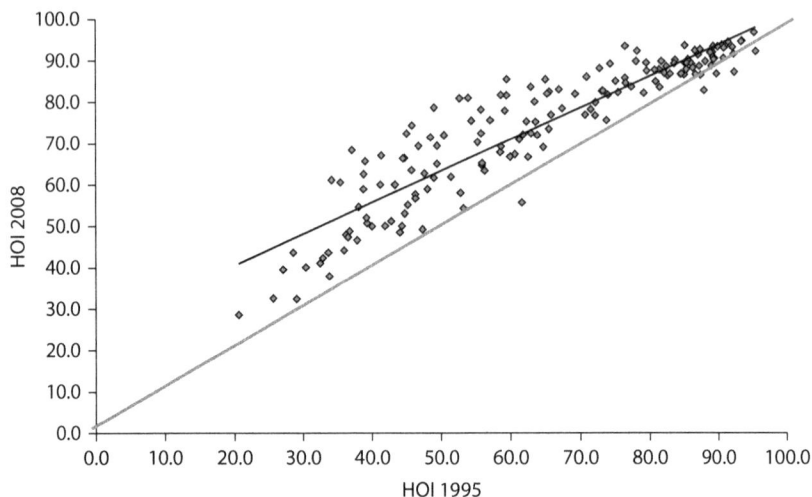

Source: Authors' calculations using SEDLAC data.

educational, and housing HOIs is a useful summary statistic that reflects regional differences in access to key goods and services. The standard deviation is weighted by the population share of each location to avoid biasing the indicator toward small and very unequal regions, considering that some countries have more regions or subnational governments than others.

When countries have near-universal coverage of access to basic services, such as Argentina, Chile, or Uruguay, they also have relatively low dispersion in their SN HOIs. Countries with lower HOIs show a wider disparity across SN HOIs. The countries with the highest dispersion in the sample between the two periods are Honduras, Nicaragua, and Peru with dispersion values of 15 to 21, followed by Colombia, Dominican Republic, El Salvador, Guatemala, and Paraguay with dispersion values between 10 and 15. Countries with the lowest dispersion are, as expected, Argentina, Chile, Costa Rica, and Uruguay. One exception is Peru, with the highest dispersion circa 1995 and yet an HOI just below the mean.

SN HOIs show a degree of convergence, as countries expand and equalize human opportunities as they develop. Countries with low HOIs tend to have a larger spread of SN HOIs, whereas countries with a higher national HOI have a lower subnational spread. The dispersion of SN HOIs tends to be higher, the lower the national-level index (figure 4.8). In this sense, achieving more coverage with more equality over time tends

Figure 4.8   Dispersion of HOI circa 1995 and 2008

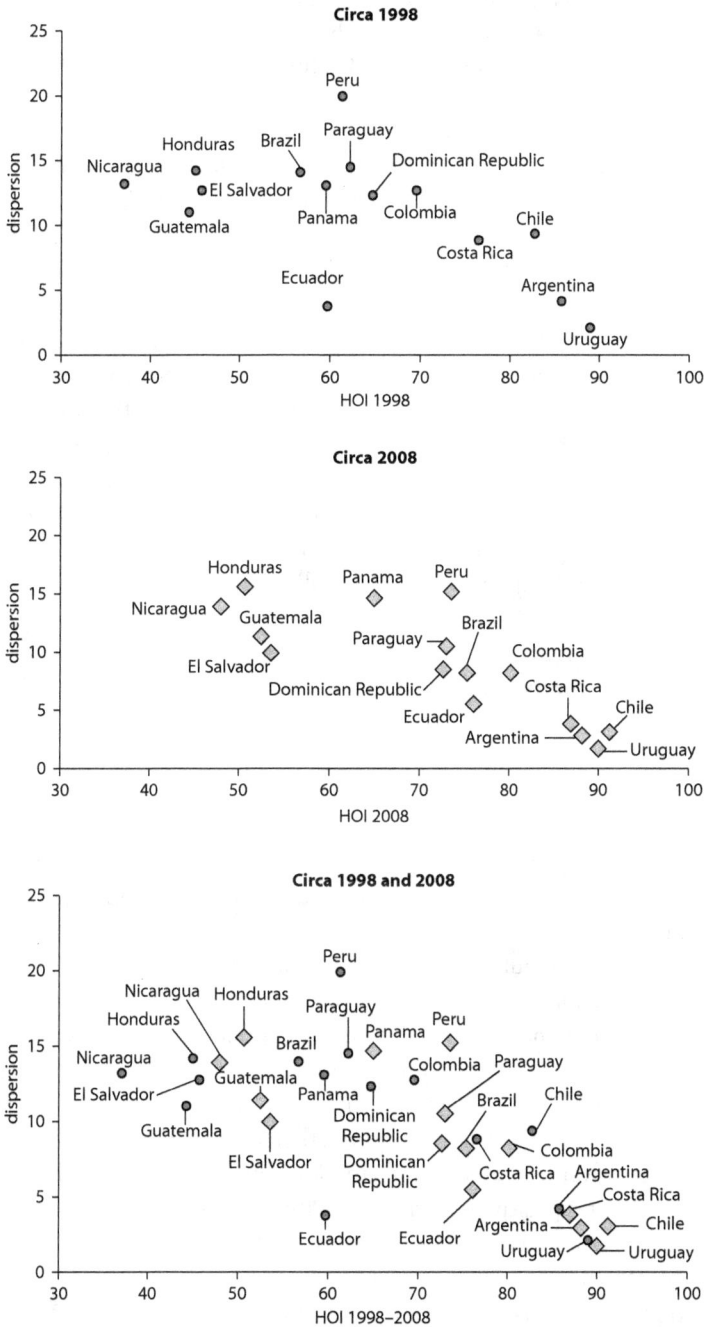

Source: Authors' calculations using SEDLAC data.

to close regional disparities in opportunities. In most countries the dispersion in SN HOIs decreased between circa 1995 and 2008, except in Ecuador, Guatemala, Honduras, Nicaragua, and Panama, where it increased even though the overall HOI for those countries improved during the period (figure 4.9).

Do Federal Countries Equalize HOIs More than Unitary Countries?

It is clear from the previous subsection that Latin American countries have had some convergence in the dispersion of their SN HOIs, that regions with the lowest levels of access to services tend to improve faster than the more favorable regions, and that countries with the highest (lowest) national HOIs have the lowest (highest) spread in their SN HOIs.[10] In this section, we inquire whether other factors help explain why some countries have more disparities than others, controlling for the level of their national HOI. The analysis focuses in particular on decentralization as a possible explanatory factor. Because several countries that are not formally federal have decentralized expenditures as much or in some cases more than federal countries, the analysis considers both political and expenditure decentralization.

The literature on fiscal federalism has developed interesting hypotheses on whether federal countries tend to have less or more regional disparities than more unitary systems. Proponents of decentralization maintain that the potential threat of disunion in federal states generates an incentive to reduce regional disparities, and hence federal countries are expected to have less disparity.[11] As well, local governments—being closer to the public—will have better information and thus will be able to ensure better provision of public services such as education and housing. Decentralization supporters also argue that centralized policy making often favors particular regions or cities and burdens all regions with uniform policies and public services too unresponsive to local needs and conditions, thus increasing spatial inequality.

On the other hand, flexibility in choosing policy instruments is curtailed by the division of powers in a federation. Central governments in unitary states are relatively unconstrained in their choice of appropriate policy instruments and hence might be more efficient in diminishing inequalities. Further, the advantage of local information could be outweighed by economies of scale and positive externalities with large-scale service provision by a central government. Critics of decentralization argue that a central government can more easily redistribute resources from more to less advantaged regions and has an interest in providing public services and policies

Figure 4.9 Decrease of Regional Dispersion in Most Countries

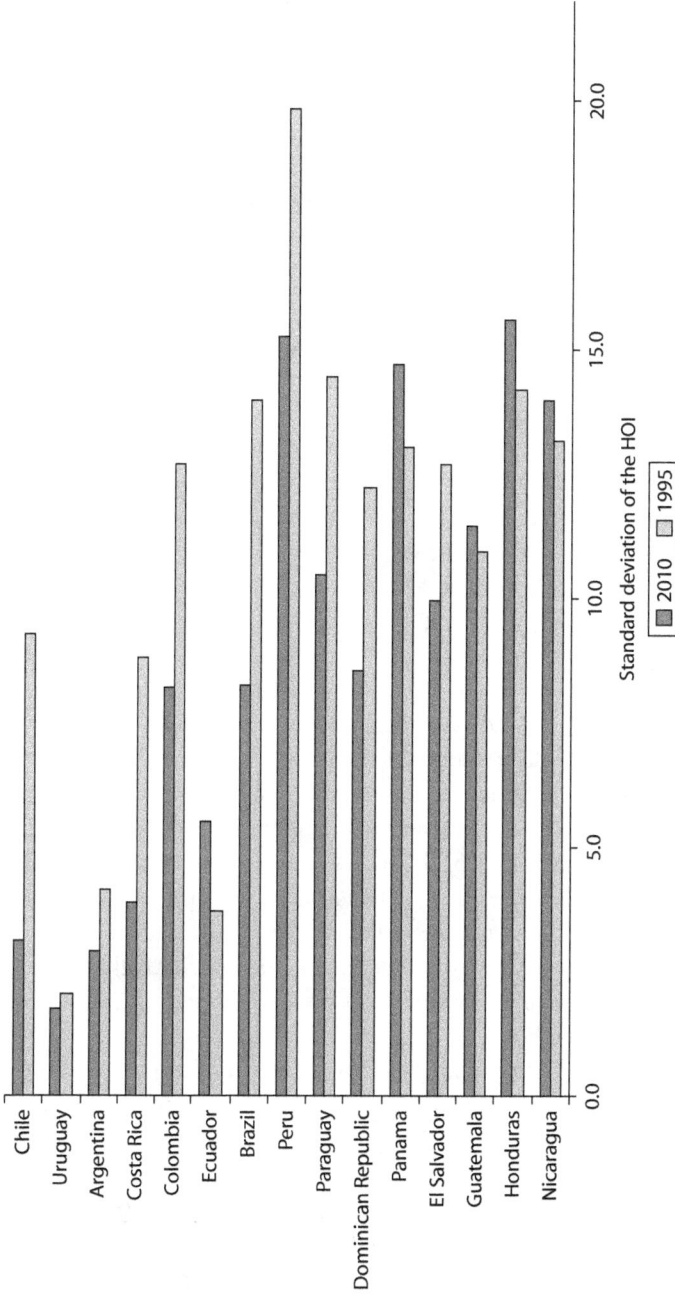

Standard deviation of the HOI

2010 ■ 1995 □

Source: Authors' calculations using SEDLAC data.
Note: Countries ordered by HOI.

equally across the country.[12] Some authors (Burki, Perry, and Dillinger 1999) also claim that decentralizing expenditure can shift power from national to local elites and might act as an incentive for corruption at the local level and limit improvements in local services provision.

In the past few decades, Latin America has undergone a major decentralization process, involving institutional, fiscal, and political reforms. The process has differed from country to country, not only in the intensity and depth of the reforms, but also in their outcomes (table 4.1). Only two formally federal countries in the sample of LAC countries are considered: Argentina and Brazil. That said, the rest of the countries under study have elections at least at the municipal level, offering some elements of decentralized political systems.

With respect to fiscal federalism, the experience is more varied. Some countries have a high level of decentralization on the expenditure side, such as Argentina, Brazil, and Colombia, whereas other countries such as Chile, Costa Rica, and El Salvador are much more centralized. The process of fiscal decentralization on the revenue side is not as deep as on the expenditure side. Except for Argentina and Brazil, most LAC countries do not raise significant amounts of subnational taxes. Also, data on subnational revenues are much less accurate than subnational expenditure data. As a result, we use subnational expenditure data to measure the extent of fiscal decentralization.[13] Expenditure data, being continuous in nature, more accurately reflect the fact that decentralization is not an "all-or-nothing" phenomenon, and that countries exist along a continuum of reform.

The analysis of the relationship between political and fiscal federalism and regional inequality of opportunity is preliminary, suggesting possible areas for further research. To test the hypothesis as to whether decentralization increases or decreases spatial dispersion in the HOI, we run linear regressions with the variability measure as the dependent variable, and as independent variables the log of the national overall HOI, the formal index of federalism or alternatively the log of expenditure measure of decentralization, and the log size of the country (in square kilometers).

A caveat worth mentioning is that decentralization is complex and most countries have diverse institutions and arrangements, and the use of quantitative methods with a small number of control variables runs the risk of simplification. This explains the heavy reliance on case studies and qualitative methods in the decentralization literature. However, cross-national analysis can provide insights into how concepts and theory translate into practice, and it can indicate general trends that might

Table 4.1   Federalism in Selected Countries of Latin America

Country	Formally	Dummy formal	Subnational government spending/ total government spending 1995	Subnational government spending/ total government spending 2004
Argentina	Federal	1	49.3	49.3
Bolivia	Unitary	0	26.7	25.1
Brazil	Federal	1	45.6	47.0
Chile	Unitary	0	13.6	12.8
Colombia	Unitary	0	39.0	44.7
Costa Rica	Unitary	0	2.3	3.1
Dominican Republic	Unitary	0	3.2	3.2
Ecuador	Unitary	0	7.5	17.5
El Salvador	Unitary	0	6.0	5.1
Guatemala	Unitary	0	10.3	10.3
Honduras	Unitary	0	12.3	12.3
Nicaragua	Unitary	0	5.2	5.0
Panama	Unitary	0	2.9	1.0
Paraguay	Unitary	0	6.2	4.0
Peru	Unitary	0	10.5	19.0
Uruguay	Unitary	0	14.2	13.7
Venezuela, R. B.	Federal	1	19.6	19.6

Source: Stein (1999) and update by Daughters and Harper (2007).

otherwise be masked. Although cross-national studies do not provide country-specific policy prescriptions, they can improve our understanding of how phenomena such as decentralization work in general terms and are useful when interpreted in this light.[14]

The econometric results suggest lower levels of regional dispersion are correlated with higher HOI levels, greater expenditure decentralization, and smaller land areas (table 4.2). Although the data are limited and further analysis is warranted, the results also indicate that federal systems are associated with lower levels of regional dispersion. This is true using either a specification based on government expenditure or one based on a political definition, although the latter is significant only at the 10 percent level (columns 1 and 2, table 4.2). As expected, the higher the HOI index, the lower the dispersion: The coefficient is negative and statistically significant at the 1 percent level. The log of area has a positive and statistically significant coefficient at the 5 percent level in both specifications of columns 1 and 2, meaning the larger the land size of the country, the more likely it is that the dispersion in basic goods and services is also larger. Hence, it appears more difficult for larger countries to equalize basic goods and services for the same level of development and decentralization.[15]

A country's land area is less significantly associated with the education HOI than with the housing HOI, suggesting that it is less difficult to bring educational opportunities to remote areas than housing opportunities. The size of the country is positively associated with inequality only in the case of housing and appears less relevant in the distribution of educational opportunities across locations. Expenditure decentralization does not appear to exert significant influence on the spread of housing opportunities across locations, but it does seem to exert a negative and significant effect on the education HOI, significant at the 5 percent level.[16] Here, too, political federalism seems to be negatively correlated with the extent of regional inequality in accessing housing and education opportunities, although again these results are tentative and call for further research.

Fiscal decentralization seems associated with lower regional dispersion of HOIs, and especially of educational HOIs. Most countries in Latin America have decentralized schooling systems for at least a significant share of education responsibilities (only Costa Rica, Ecuador, Panama, Paraguay, and Uruguay retain centralized educational systems). However, even in LAC countries that have decentralized primary education, the central government retains functions at the national level (Burki, Perry, and Dillinger 1999).

Table 4.2   OLS Estimates Subnational Dispersion in HOIs
weighted standard deviation

	All opportunities		Housing opportunities		Education opportunities	
	(1)	(2)	(3)	(4)	(5)	(6)
Federal	−6.5044**		−7.6218**	−3.7787*		
	(−2.61)		(−2.09)		(−1.84)	
Subspend		−1.9492*		−1.7374		−1.7979**
		(−1.85)		(−1.13)		(−2.25)
lnArea	1.3765**	1.4244**	1.9282**	1.7281*	0.4801	0.8306
	(2.54)	(2.07)	(2.47)	(1.74)	(1.08)	(1.62)
lnHOIj	−14.5857***	−15.0744***	−13.1582***	−13.7144***	−10.3580***	−10.5387***
	(−5.93)	(−5.77)	(−5.53)	(−5.47)	(−3.94)	(−4.11)
Constant	64.2908***	69.6409***	58.1717***	64.4961***	48.7070***	51.1109***
	(6.51)	(6.77)	(6.08)	(6.79)	(4.51)	(4.83)
N	30	30	30	30	30	30
r^2	0.6235	0.5799	0.5908	0.5445	0.4165	0.4481
F	14.3544	11.9619	12.5105	10.3595	6.1859	7.0376

Source: Authors' calculations using SEDLAC data and data in table 4.1.
Note: Columns 1 and 2, which show the estimates for the overall HOI constructed from the average of the five basic housing and education opportunities, differ only in the control used to proxy federalism, which is based on a political definition or empirical government expenditure.
t statistics in parentheses. *$p < 0.10$; **$p < 0.05$; ***$p < 0.01$.

In the case of housing infrastructure, responsibilities are shared among national, provincial, and state levels and with state or private enterprises, often creating accountability and responsibility problems in the provision of water, sanitation, and electricity. As noted by Foster (2005), the decentralization of water and sanitation services to small local governments in LAC led to a loss of economies of scale in service delivery in countries such as Argentina, Colombia, and Peru, entailing a sudden fragmentation of the industry into hundreds of small municipal providers. In several cases, decentralization preceded subsequent water sector reform by many years. This lack of synchronicity between structural and regulatory reform was unfortunate because it meant that regulatory reform had to be superimposed on an industry structure that was often far from optimal in an economic sense. Hence, it might be that well-coordinated and managed expenditure decentralization even in the case of housing might help equalize housing opportunities.[17]

This analysis suggests that fiscal decentralization may have been more effective in diminishing regional inequalities in the case of education than in the case of sanitation, water, or electricity. At a minimum, it is clear that equalizing housing and education opportunities will require different policies in each sector, although there are common policy principles, as discussed in the next section.

We conclude that significant regional inequalities persist in many LAC countries. By most measures of regional inequality, countries with lower access to basic goods and services tend to have more regional dispersion, but also tend to experience higher rates of improvement in the index, demonstrating a growing regional convergence in the provision of basic goods and services. Some evidence indicates that more fiscally decentralized countries achieve less HOI disparity, at least in terms of education.[18] But large dispersions still need to be addressed to level the playing field for children born in different locations.

Equalizing Regional Opportunities

The *World Development Report 2009* (World Bank 2009b) calls for countries to equalize basic opportunities across provinces and states, rather than trying to equalize outcomes such as GDP or poverty rates. Hence, the objective is not only reaching universal coverage of basic opportunities, but also ensuring that, until universal coverage is achieved, the distribution of access to basic services should be equalized across regions. Policy measures can assist countries to achieve greater fiscal equity and redistribute government expenditure to more unequal regions. The problem is to find the best and most efficient approach in LAC, given concerns over public sector accountability and in light of the predominance of hybrid political structures (neither clearly federal nor unitary) where functions tend to be superimposed and not always clearly defined.

Decentralization seems irreversible in LAC countries, so a possible way to help accelerate the reduction in regional disparities could be to design an equal opportunity policy coordinated by the central government and implemented at the subnational level. Local governments in all LAC countries rely at least partially on transfers from central governments, so this policy could take the form of an "equal opportunity grant" transfer from central to local governments to mitigate inequality in accessing opportunities. This would involve distributing, on a per capita basis, resources to provinces that attain specific goals in access to education, health, and sanitation. The HOI is an ideal index to measure performance under conditional grants aimed at leveling the playing field in accessing opportunities, because it is straightforward to estimate given widely available household data in LAC and has clear interpretations.

In the 1980s and 1990s, many countries in Latin America introduced fiscal grants to subnational governments to support decentralization. Some of these programs were conditional on inputs (classroom construction, teacher salaries). However, input conditionality undermines budgetary autonomy and flexibility without providing any assurance of achieving results.[19] Hence, the proposal is that the grant should be conditioned on attaining equitably distributed access to basic services; that is, the grant would be more concerned with outputs rather than with inputs. A growing number of countries are implementing transfer programs conditioned on attaining particular opportunities across states or regions: the Australian National Schools Specific Purpose Payments, the Canadian Health Transfers program, the Brazilian Unified Heath System and the FUNDEF program for primary schooling, and Chile's grants to municipal governments for water and sewer access for the poor (Shah 2010).

Some have suggested that the move in recent years to output-based budgeting in place of input-based budgeting should be mirrored by a shift toward performance-based grants, particularly for capital grants (Steffensen and Larsen 2005). In contrast, Smart and Bird (2009) claim performance-based grants cannot work for most intergovernmental systems. They maintain that there may be a limited role for a "reward" system of grants, in which those who perform best get the most. Given that most local governments depend on secure (precommitted) grant funding to carry out many activities, and that many grant programs are intended to meet "needs" rather than to reward those who have already succeeded in doing so, performance-based budgeting may be challenging to implement.

Hence, although output- and performance-based grants are clearly superior incentives for local governments to help provide opportunities for accessing key goods and services, "penalties" can be hard to sustain in the face of precommitted funds designed to provide access to basic services. Some authors propose a form of conditional grant, without curtailing precommitted funds but with public exposure of performance. In Australia, the National School Program is part of an overall reporting and accountability framework, and states must provide performance data to the Commonwealth and to the general public. A continuous and independent dissemination of the estimation of the HOI across subregions could be fundamental in improving performance and accountability without hurting citizens.

In contrast, the United States enacted a highly conditional national education program in 2001 through the *No Child Left Behind* Act. This act transfers funds from the federal government and requires states to establish goals for all students and for groups of students characterized by race, ethnicity, poverty, disability, and limited English proficiency, and requires schools to make annual progress in meeting these goals. If goals are not met as determined by test standards, the school and the state are subject to sanctions.[20] If the performance of local governments and schools does not improve, transfers can be made directly to the individual, making sure his or her opportunities are enhanced.

Although *No Child Left Behind* has been controversial, Hanushek and Raymond (2005) find that, despite flaws, the act has a positive impact on achievement. However, the impact holds just for states attaching consequences to performance.[21] This is an important finding to take into account for countries designing an equal opportunity grant. The authors also found that, although the grant increased average performance, the performance of blacks increased more slowly than whites, hence widening the black–white education achievement gap. If the HOI for educational achievement were estimated based on the standardized achievement test (as in chapter 3), and if grants are conditional on these indices, some of the problems associated with inequality in the increased achievement scores could be avoided.

Along these lines, the *World Development Report 2009* (World Bank 2009b) stressed the need for "collecting and disseminating credible information on service entitlements to increase the accountability of service providers and improve outcomes" at the subnational level. Collecting HOIs periodically can serve this purpose, and they are an optimal index to target and condition federal grants, at minimum by publicizing performance. Until now, the only data available have been on poverty rates, income per capita, and other outcome measures. Although useful, these cannot help policies that focus on improving equitable access to basic services, such that children in poorer regions have equal access to opportunities that are critical to allow them to develop their potential.

Based on the stylized facts about the evolution of HOIs for different opportunities and across regions, the available literature on grant design and expenditure decentralization, and the institutional and political context in most LAC countries, several principles should be considered for equal opportunity grants:

- The grant can be distributed to different levels of government depending on the specific institutional structure of the country—unitary, federal, or myriad intermediate options. Functions and responsibilities of each level of government in equalizing opportunities should be assigned clearly. In the case of housing, and to some extent in education, responsibilities are often shared among national, provincial, and state bodies as well as private enterprises. This mixed approach to service delivery can create problems of accountability and quality, possibly explaining the lack of better results in equalizing basic service opportunities across regions.

- The expenditure "need" for each opportunity to access a key good or service should be calculated. The cost is likely to vary inversely with the specific coverage rate and directly with inequality of opportunity: In more remote locations, the cost per capita is expected to be higher; it is also expected that other circumstances such as family education or family income would be lower for those locations, and hence the need to equalize with even higher expenditure per capita.

- For ease of monitoring and implementation, the grants should be divided by key good or service. Canada enacted in 1996 a joint conditional grant (CHST) for health, education, and social minimum standards of coverage and insurance by province but later subdivided it to better monitor compliance and better calculate amounts for each key good or service.

- The grant is not meant to replace an equalization transfer. As noted by Vaillancourt and Bird (2005), the central aim of an equalization transfer is to *enable* subnational governments with different abilities to raise revenues to provide comparable levels of services. Because no country is completely uniform, a fundamental characteristic of a decentralized state is that subnational governments have different fiscal capacities and are unable to provide the same level of public services at the same tax rates. Equalization transfers are mostly unconditional and thus permit regional differences. The equal opportunity grant can complement equalization transfers by conditioning the grant on actually attaining national target goals for service-equitable service provision. In fact, the central government in Canada has two main transfers, the unconditional equalization transfer and the CHST, a major conditional transfer to guarantee horizontal equity. Australia also has a conditional grant called Specific Purpose Payments (SPPs) and a formal equalization program that is mostly unconditional. About half of transfers are through the SPPs to achieve national policy objectives, mainly for education and health care.

- This type of grant would be better as a performance-based grant rather than one conditioned on inputs. The grant should be conditional on gradually attaining equality of opportunity across locations and within each location. It should reward good performers and penalize bad performers, without punishing inhabitants. The government should be liable, not the individual. To achieve this, each country should evaluate the advantages and disadvantages of conditionality ranging from a minimum of publicizing results up to enacting penalties of varying degrees.

- Whatever conditionality is employed, the systematic collection, analysis, and reporting of information is important to verify compliance with stated goals and to assist future decisions (Bird 2000). Unless central agencies monitor and evaluate local performance, there can be no assurance that nationally important goods and services are adequately provided once they have been decentralized. An important part of any decentralization program is thus improved national evaluation capacity.

- Above all, a widely publicized commitment to leveling the playing field across all regions of the country is essential. All individuals should be aware of this and should periodically receive data on the progress of different local governments in achieving the agreed goals. When public commitment or enthusiasm wanes and conditionality becomes lax, then the grant ends up becoming an unconditional grant without any result or improvement (see Zanetta 2004 for an example).

Summary and Conclusions

This chapter estimates a series of subnational Human Opportunity Indices (SN HOIs) using data from 30 household surveys for 15 LAC countries over a period of more than a decade (1995–2009). Together, the surveys represent more than 160 subregions. Using the same opportunities for accessing key services, circumstances, and overall methodology as in chapter 2 for building the national indices, the chapter seeks to uncover basic stylized facts on regional inequality of opportunities and outlines a possible instrument to redress this inequality. The main findings are the following:

- The range for SN HOIs is much higher than the range of national HOIs: from 97 for Tierra del Fuego, Argentina, to 29 in the Atlantic Region, Nicaragua, and the indigenous Comarcas, Panama. Capital cities tended to have higher HOIs than the rest of their respective countries. Moreover, the higher the HOI, the narrower the gap between access to opportunities in capital cities and the rest of the country.

- Overall, disparities in accessing basic services within most LAC countries reflect differences in housing SN HOIs more than differences in education SN HOIs. Housing SN HOIs have a higher range than education SN HOIs, and the differences between capital cities and the rest of the country are much more pronounced for housing than for education. All capital cities ranked better than the rest of the country for housing, but this was not always the case for education.

- Access to basic services appears to be converging over time within regions of a country. The highest increases in the HOIs were attained mostly by subregions with the lowest initial HOI, and the lowest growth was attained by the capitals (mostly of high HOI countries, such as Argentina, Chile, Colombia, and Costa Rica). A strong negative and statistically significant relationship was found between the rate of growth of the 165 SN HOIs and the initial level of the SN HOI. This convergence was stronger in the case of the education HOI, suggesting that it is more challenging to level the playing field in housing compared with education.

- Subregional differences in accessing key services tend to decrease as the overall level of the HOI increases. In most countries the dispersion in the SN HOIs decreased between circa 1995 and 2008. Moreover, after measuring inequality in SN HOIs among subregions through the weighted standard deviation, countries with the highest HOI tended to have the lowest dispersion. Because the average education HOI is higher than the average housing HOI, less dispersion was seen in the education HOI than in the housing HOI.

- Higher HOIs, expenditure decentralization, and small country size are associated with less subregional HOI dispersion. Although the data were not conclusive, the data suggest that political decentralization may also be correlated with more regional equality.

To help level the playing field, the chapter offers guiding principles to design a performance-based "equal opportunity" grant. This grant would promote government accountability and would help ensure that children in each province receive equal opportunities to access basic services, thereby accelerating convergence toward universal coverage.

Annex

Table A4.1 Countries, Provinces, or Subregions and Years

Country	Survey years		Provinces	Subregions
Argentina	1998	2008	23	
Brazil	1995	2008	27	
Chile	1996	2006	13	
Colombia	1997	2008	9	
Costa Rica	1994	2009		6
Dominican Republic	2000	2008		9
Ecuador	1995	2006		3
El Salvador	1998	2007	14	
Guatemala	2000	2006		8
Honduras	1999	2007		4
Nicaragua	1998	2005		4
Panama	1997	2003	9	
Paraguay	1999	2008	9	
Peru	1998	2008		7
Uruguay	2006	2008	19	
Total			123	42

Source: World Bank and Universidad de La Plata (CEDLAS) Socioeconomic Database for Latin America and the Caribbean.
Note: The provinces and subregions used here are only those with representative data available.

Table A4.2 Subnational HOIs, 2008

Ranking	Region	HOI	Ranking	Region	HOI
1	Tierra del Fuego, Argentina	97	25	Rocha, Uruguay	90
2	Antofagasta, Chile	95	26	San Luis, Argentina	90
3	Bogotá, Distrito Capital, Colombia	95	27	Central, Costa Rica	90
4	Mendoza, Argentina	95	28	Catamarca, Argentina	90
5	Tarapacá, Chile	94	29	Magallanes y la Antártida Chilena, Chile	90
6	Atacama, Chile	94	30	Corrientes, Argentina	90
7	Metropolitana de Santiago, Chile	94	31	Libertador General B . O'Higgins, Chile	90
8	Salta, Argentina	94	32	Valle del Cauca, Colombia	89
9	Región Aysén del General Carlos Ibáñez del Campo, Chile	94	33	Cerro Largo, Uruguay	89
10	Chubut, Argentina	93	34	Lima metropolitana, Peru	89
11	Florida, Uruguay	93	35	Río Negro, Uruguay	89
12	Santa Cruz, Argentina	93	36	Bio-Bio, Chile	89
13	Maldonado, Uruguay	93	37	Treinta y tres, Uruguay	89
14	Valparaíso, Chile	93	38	Salto, Uruguay	89
15	Córdoba, Argentina	92	39	Entre Ríos, Argentina	89
16	Coquimbo, Chile	92	40	Tacuarembó, Uruguay	88
17	City of Buenos Aires, Argentina	92	41	Maule, Chile	88
18	Neuquén, Argentina	92	42	Artigas, Uruguay	88
19	Soriano, Uruguay	92	43	La Rioja, Argentina	88
20	Colonia, Uruguay	92	44	Orinoquia y Amazonia, Colombia	88
21	La Pampa, Argentina	91	45	Chaco, Argentina	88
22	Canelones, Uruguay	91	46	Flores, Uruguay	87
23	Montevideo, Uruguay	91	47	Santa Fe, Argentina	87
24	Durazno, Uruguay	91	48	Tucumán, Argentina	87

(continued next page)

Table A4.2 *(continued)*

Ranking	Region	HOI	Ranking	Region	HOI
49	Rivera , Uruguay	87	73	Huetar Atlántica, Costa Rica	82
50	La Valleja, Uruguay	87	74	Rio Grande du Sul, Brazil	82
51	Jujuy, Argentina	87	75	Misiones, Argentina	82
52	San Jose, Uruguay	87	76	Sierra,[a] Ecuador	82
53	Buenos Aires, Argentina	87	77	Oriental, Colombia	82
54	Paysandú, Uruguay	87	78	Goiás, Brazil	81
55	Formosa, Argentina	86	79	Mato Grosso Sul, Brazil	81
56	Los Lagos, Chile	86	80	Huetar Norte, Costa Rica	80
57	Costa urbana, Peru	86	81	Central, Colombia	80
58	Paraná, Brazil	86	82	Mato Grosso, Brazil	79
59	Brunca, Costa Rica	86	83	Antioquia, Colombia	79
60	São Paulo, Brazil	85	84	Región Norcentral, Dominican Republic	78
61	San Juan, Argentina	85	85	Minas Gerais, Brazil	78
62	Sierra urbana, Peru	85	86	Espirito Santo, Brazil	78
63	Araucania, Chile	84	87	Rio de Janeiro, Brazil	77
64	Central, Paraguay	84	88	Selva urbana, Peru	77
65	Santiago del Estero, Argentina	84	89	San Pedro Sula, Honduras	77
66	Santa Catarina, Brazil	83	90	Panamá, Panamá	76
67	Asunción, Paraguay	83	91	Colón, Panamá	76
68	Pacífico Central, Costa Rica	83	92	Amapá, Brazil	75
69	Distrito federal, Brazil	83	93	Roraima, Brazil	75
70	Chorotega, Costa Rica	83	94	Región Cibao Central, Dominican Republic	75
71	San Andrés y Providencia, Colombia	82	95	Paraguarí, Paraguay	74
72	Región Distrito Nacional, Dominican Republic	82	96	Tegucigalpa (Distrito Nacional), Honduras	74

97	Cordillera, Paraguay	72
98	Rio Grande du Norte, Brazil	72
99	Costa, Ecuador	72
100	Rondonia, Brazil	72
101	Sergipe, Brazil	72
102	Metropolitana, Guatemala	72
103	Alto Paraná, Paraguay	72
104	Atlántica, Colombia	71
105	Pacífica, Colombia	70
106	Chiriquí, Panamá	69
107	Paraíba, Brazil	69
108	Managua, Nicaragua	69
109	San Salvador, El Salvador	69
110	Ceará, Brazil	68
111	Amazonas, Brazil	68
112	Herrera, Panamá	67
113	Bahia, Brazil	67
114	Región Este, Dominican Republic	67
115	Región Noroeste, Dominican Republic	67
116	Pernambuco, Brazil	67
117	Región Nordeste, Dominican Republic	66
118	Tocantins, Brazil	66
119	Remaining Urban Areas, Honduras	65
120	Para, Brazil	65
121	Región Valdesia, Dominican Republic	65
122	Oriente/Amazonia, Ecuador	64
123	Caaguazú, Paraguay	63
124	San Pedro, Paraguay	63
125	Alagoas, Brazil	63
126	Los Santos, Panamá	62
127	Guairá, Paraguay	62
128	Maranhao, Brazil	61
129	Piauí, Brazil	61
130	Costa rural, Peru	60
131	Región del Valle, Dominican Republic	60
132	Sierra rural, Peru	59
133	Coclé, Panamá	59
134	Acre, Brazil	58
135	Central, Guatemala	58
136	Bocas del toro, Panamá	57
137	Región Enriquillo, Dominican Republic	56
138	La Libertad, El Salvador	55
139	Pacífico, Nicaragua	55
140	Itapúa, Paraguay	54
141	Suroccidente, Guatemala	53
142	Santa Ana, El Salvador	52
143	Chalatenango, El Salvador	51
144	La Paz, El Salvador	51
145	Veraguas, Panamá	50
146	San Vicente, El Salvador	50
147	Nororiente, Guatemala	50
148	Cuscatlán, El Salvador	49
149	Usulután, El Salvador	49
150	Suroriente, Guatemala	49
151	Sonsonate, El Salvador	48
152	Rural Forest, Peru	47

(continued next page)

Table A4.2 *(continued)*

Ranking	Region	HOI	Ranking	Region	HOI
153	San Miguel, El Salvador	47	160	Central, Nicaragua	40
154	Noroccidente, Guatemala	44	161	Rural, Honduras	38
155	Cabañas, El Salvador	44	162	Norte, Guatemala	33
156	Ahuachapán, El Salvador	44	163	Morazán, El Salvador	33
157	La Unión, El Salvador	42	164	Indigenous Comarcas, Panamá	29
158	Darién, Panamá	41	165	Atlántico, Nicaragua	29
159	Petén, Guatemala	40			

Source: World Bank and Universidad de La Plata (CEDLAS) Socioeconomic Database Survey years for Latin America and the Caribbean.

a. Includes Quito, the capital city.

Notes

1. The heterogeneity in the data are corrected to the extent possible in next sections. A sensitivity analysis of the results was done by grouping all the countries by region and not by province. Although minor changes will be noted in the following sections, most conclusions remain unchanged.

2. In this chapter the terms regional, subnational, provincial, or state government are used interchangeably unless specified, for example, between provinces and municipalities, which are clearly two different government levels. Some of the countries analyzed in chapter 2 did not have representative data at any regional or subnational level and hence were dropped from this analysis (see table A4.1). This is the case for Bolivia, Jamaica, Mexico, and República Bolivariana de Venezuela. Among the 15 remaining countries, seven—Costa Rica, Dominican Republic, Ecuador, Guatemala, Honduras, Nicaragua, and Peru—could not be analyzed by province or department because the data were not representative at that level of analysis, and hence regional data were divided into economic or natural regions by the respective national statistics institutes. The rest of the countries were divided across provinces or departments. However, in some cases, such as Paraguay, the departments included may not cover all the national territory and population, because their sample size was not sufficiently high to estimate the HOI. The standard error of the SN HOIs is much larger than that of the national HOIs because their sample size is obviously much smaller. In this respect, the ranking among SN HOIs should be analyzed with care.

3. This analysis is not strict, not only because of heterogeneity in the definition of subregions but also because countries have different numbers of subregions, whatever the definition used. Nonetheless, the comparisons are revealing.

4. According to the latest data available in "World Development Indicators 2009" (World Bank 2009a), the Gini coefficient for per capita income was 55 for Brazil in 2007 and 58.5 for Colombia in 2006. ECLAC (2008) classifies Brazil and Colombia within the "high inequality" countries in LAC, together with Bolivia, Guatemala, and Honduras. It also notes that, although income inequality in Brazil decreased in the 2000s, the opposite occurred in Colombia. With respect to regional inequality, Herrán (2005) found that in 2000 in Brazil, 24 percent of income inequality was explained by regional differences, and 76 percent was due to household-specific characteristics. Colombia, in spite of perceptions of high regional disparities in income (measured by gross national product), is not highly unequal as measured by the HOI, but rather moderate compared internationally. However, it does not show convergence among its regions or policies to diminish regional inequalities.

5. Comparisons between the capital city and the rest of the country reflect in part the wide differences between urban and rural HOIs, but also the high disparities in LAC between main capital cities—usually megacities, modern,

but with an important agglomeration of inhabitants, migrants, and slums, and with economic activity centralized around the metropolitan area—and other "provincial" cities.

6. Brasilia might rank at the top because of its relatively "new" status as capital. Nonetheless, the same ranking holds if Rio de Janeiro or São Paulo are used (with a housing HOI of 95 and 97 percent, respectively).

7. The decrease in the annual growth in services in some of the cities should be interpreted with care. The sample size and problems with the comparability of the data, especially in the case of Argentina and Paraguay, might be driving the negative result. Most likely the rate of growth in these capitals should be close to zero.

8. A simple OLS regression of the 165 SN HOIs rate of growth and the HOIs estimates a coefficient of −0.015 and a t-statistic of −4.67, showing the coefficient to be statistically significant in explaining that regions with more limited opportunities grow on average at faster rates than higher ranked regions.

9. Even if policy makers could control regional outcomes, the *World Development Report 2009* (World Bank 2009b) asserts that it is not efficient to equalize geographical GDP. Instead, people in different regions can be empowered to move if desired to regions with more dynamic economic activity.

10. The literature on geographical GDP convergence (see Barro and Sala-i-Martin 1991) distinguishes two types of convergence in growth: sigma convergence and beta convergence. A falling dispersion of real per capita income across a group of economies over time signifies sigma convergence, and a negative partial correlation between growth in income over time and its initial level signifies beta convergence. Hence, in the case of the HOI there is both sigma convergence—because there is a reduction in the dispersion of SN HOIs—as well as beta convergence that produces faster growth in regions with lower coverage, corrected for inequality opportunities. Some authors also showed that beta convergence is necessary for sigma convergence.

11. Decentralization can also increase regional disparities between jurisdictions. Prud'homme (1994, 1996) argues that decentralized redistribution is likely to lead to different treatment of similar individuals in a country. For example, jurisdictions with higher per capita income would be able to provide higher levels of public services than those with lower per capita income. Residents in wealthier jurisdictions could even be levied at lower tax rates for higher levels of public services than those in poor jurisdictions.

12. See Faguet and Shami (2008) for an excellent exposition of advantages and disadvantages of decentralization in promoting regional equality.

13. We use the decentralization data gathered by the International Development Bank through a series of interviews, used by Stein (1999) and updated by

Daughters and Harper (2007), so we can relate this index to measures of dispersion in 1995 and 2008 to test our hypothesis.

14. Another problem in a cross section without a long time series is that country-specific unobserved variables can bias and confound interpretation of coefficients. Control variables in part mitigate these effects.

15. The log of population was also used as a control variable alternative to the size of the country. Its coefficient was positive as expected, but not statistically significant. The coefficient on the political dummy for federalism is negative and statistically significant at the 5 percent level, meaning that federal countries have a lower dispersion in the level of overall opportunities corrected for inequalities. However, only two countries in the sample are federal (the sample for regions or subnational areas in República Bolivariana de Venezuela, the other federal country, was not representative for estimating the HOIs and had to be dropped). Hence, this dummy is only for Argentina and Brazil and thus could be confounding the effect of just federalism (although size in the sample is already controlled by the log of surface area).

16. There is a small number of observations ($N = 30$) to perform tests only asymptotically valid to analyze further the statistical properties of the ordinary least squares model. However, robust and clustered standard errors were estimated for the model, resulting in similar standard errors, albeit smaller in the case of the robust option. None of the conclusions significantly changed.

17. More research needs to be done to ascertain the reasons for the lack of significance of the coefficient on decentralization for housing. Some authors such as Foster (2005) and Zannetta (2004) find that the cause of policy failure is "inadequate" decentralization without controls from the central government and a clear assignment of specific functions between local and central governments, more than decentralization per se.

18. Regressions were also run using macroregions for the countries that in table A4.1 were subdivided by provinces, and the same regions for the rest. Although the size of the dispersion changes in several cases, the results of the regression remain basically unaltered, even increasing the significance of the coefficients of some variables, such as subnational expenditure.

19. Hanushek (2003) reviewed available evidence on the effects of schooling inputs and outcomes and did not find any evidence that spending more on teachers or schools improves student outcomes.

20. A school failing to make adequate progress for three consecutive years must initiate a performance improvement plan and give students the option to move to other public schools. A fourth year of failure requires restructuring and supplemental education services. If a school fails to make progress in the fifth year, it must implement restructuring, including changes in staff and

management or converting into a semiprivate (charter) school. The district must provide transportation to the new school. The state must permit low-income students attending persistently failing schools to use special funds to obtain supplemental educational services from the public or private providers selected by the students and their parents.

21. In the authors' words, "States that simply provide better information through report cards without attaching consequences to performance do not get significantly larger impacts over no accountability" (Hanushek and Raymond 2005, 22).

Bibliography

Barro, R. J., and X. Sala-i-Martin. 1991. "Convergence across States and Regions." *Brookings Papers on Economic Activity*, 107–82.

Bird, Richard M. 2000. "Transfers and Incentives in Intergovernmental Relations." In *Decentralization and Accountability of the Public Sector*, ed. S. Burki and G. Perry. Washington, DC: World Bank.

Burki, S. J., G. Perry, and W. Dillinger. 1999. *Beyond the Center: Decentralizing the State*. Washington, DC: World Bank.

Daughters, R., and L. Harper. 2007. "Fiscal and Political Decentralization Reforms." In *The State of State Reform in Latin America*, ed. E. Lora. Stanford, CA: Stanford University Press.

ECLAC (Economic Commission for Latin America). 2008. *Panorama social de América Latina 2008*. CEPAL, Santiago de Chile.

Faguet, Jean-Paul, and Mahvish Shami. 2008. "Fiscal Policy and Spatial Inequality in Latin America and Beyond." Policy Research Working Paper Series, World Bank, Washington, DC.

Foster, Vivien. 2005. "Ten Years of Water Service Reform in Latin America: Toward an Anglo-French Model." Water Supply and Sanitation Sector Board Discussion Paper Series No. 3, World Bank, Washington, DC.

Hanushek, Eric A. 2003. "The Failure of Input-Based Schooling Policies." *Economic Journal* 113(485): F64–F98.

Hanushek, Eric A., and Margaret E. Raymond. 2004. "Does School Accountability Lead to Improved Student Performance?" Working Paper 10591, National Bureau of Economic Research, Cambridge, Ma.

Hanushek, Eric A., and Margaret E. Raymond. 2005. "Does School Accountability Lead to Improved Student Performance?" *Journal of Policy Analysis and Management* 24(2): 297–327.

Herrán, C. 2005. "Reducing Poverty and Inequality in Brazil." Economic and Social Study Series, Inter-American Development Bank, Washington, DC.

Prud'homme. Remy. 1994. "On the Dangers of Decentralization." Policy Working Paper 1252, World Bank, Washington, DC.

————. 1996. "Comment on Conflicts and Dilemmas of Decentralization by Rudolf Hommes." In *Annual Bank Conference on Development Economics 1995*, ed. Michael Bruno and Boris Pleskovic. Washington, DC: World Bank.

Shah, Anwar. 2010. "Sponsoring a Race to the Top: The Case for Results-Based Intergovernmental Finance for Merit Goods." Policy Research Working Paper No. 5172, World Bank, Washington, DC.

Shankar, Raja, and Anwar Shah. 2003. "Bridging the Economic Divide within Nations: A Scorecard on the Performance of Regional Development Policies in Reducing Regional Income Disparities." *World Development* 31(8): 1421–41.

Smart, Michael, and Richard Bird. 2009. "Earmarked Grants and Accountability in Government." Revised, October. University of Toronto.

Steffensen, Jesper, and Henrik Larsen. 2005. "Conceptual Basis for Performance Based Grant Systems and Selected International Experiences." Background paper, National Stakeholder Workshop, May 31, Kathmandu, Nepal.

Stein, Ernesto. 1999. "Fiscal Decentralization and Government Size in Latin America." *Journal of Applied Economics* 2: 357–91.

Vaillancourt, François, and Richard Bird. 2005. "Expenditure-Based Equalization Transfers." International Tax Program Papers No. 0512, International Tax Program, Institute for International Business, Joseph L. Rotman School of Management, University of Toronto.

Von Braun, J., and U. Grote. 2002. "Does Decentralization Serve the Poor?" In *Fiscal Decentralization*, ed. International Monetary Fund, 92–119. Washington, DC: Routledge Economics.

World Bank. 2009a. "World Development Indicators." www.worldbank.org.

World Bank. 2009b. *World Development Report 2009: Reshaping Economic Geography*. Washington, DC: World Bank.

Zanetta, C. 2004. *The Influence of the World Bank on National Housing and Urban Policies: A Comparison of Mexico and Argentina during the 1990s.* London: Ashgate.

Index

Boxes, figures, notes, and tables are indicated by *b*, *f*, *n*, and *t* following page numbers.

ECO-AUDIT
Environmental Benefits Statement

The World Bank is committed to preserving endangered forests and natural resources. The Office of the Publisher has chosen to print *Do Our Children Have a Chance? A Human Opportunity Report for Latin America and the Caribbean* on recycled paper with 50 percent post-consumer waste, in accordance with the recommended standards for paper usage set by the Green Press Initiative, a nonprofit program supporting publishers in using fiber that is not sourced from endangered forests. For more information, visit www.greenpressinitiative.org.

Saved:
• 3 trees
• 1 million British thermal units of total energy
• 283 pounds of net greenhouse gases (CO_2 equivalent)
• 1,276 gallons of waste water
• 81 pounds of solid waste

green
press
INITIATIVE

www.ingramcontent.com/pod-product-compliance
Lightning Source LLC
Chambersburg PA
CBHW070920270326
41927CB00011B/2651